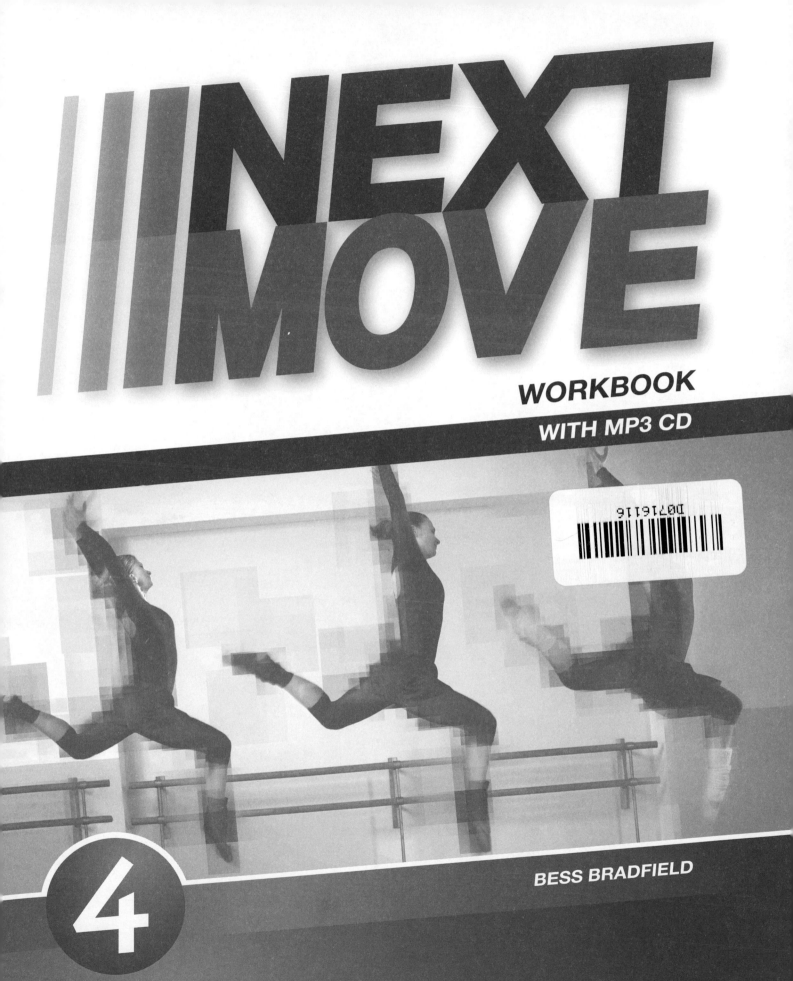

NEXT MOVE

WORKBOOK

WITH MP3 CD

4

BESS BRADFIELD

Contents

Starter Unit

Grammar and Vocabulary

to be and have got

1 Write sentences and questions. Use the correct form of *be* or *have got.*

1 My teacher / red hair ✗
My teacher hasn't got red hair.

2 I / fifteen years old ✓
....

3 your friends / any interesting hobbies ?
....
....

4 Our house / a garden ✗
....
....

5 you / afraid / of anything ?
....

6 It / sunny today ✗
....

7 My parents / a blue car ✓
....
....

8 They / hungry ✗
....

Daily routines

2 Match the verbs (1–9) to the phrases (a–i) to make daily routine collocations. Which of these things did you do yesterday?

1 walk		**a**	to school by car
2 drive		**b**	the bus
3 brush		**c**	the washing-up
4 do		**d**	your bed
5 take		**e**	the dog
6 do		**f**	a shower
7 have		**g**	your homework
8 get		**h**	dressed
9 make		**i**	your teeth

Present simple

3 Complete the conversations with the Present simple form of these verbs. Then complete the short answers.

cook	do (x2)	go	~~like~~	live	not clean	not like	play

1 **A** *Do you and your friends like* (you and your friends) shopping?
 B No, we .... shopping – it's boring! We prefer video games.

2 **A** .... (you) basketball in your free time?
 B Yes, I .... I also .... judo.

3 **A** .... (your best friend) near you?
 B No, she .... ! She .... to school in the USA – 5,000 kilometres away!

4 **A** .... (who) the housework in your home?
 B My dad always .... dinner, but he .... the house. I usually do that!

Present continuous

4 Choose the correct options. Use the Present continuous forms to complete the email.

New Message   ⊗

                                                          Send

Hi Annie,
[1] *Are you having* (you – *have / like*) a good weekend?

We [2] .... (*do / have*) a great time at the campsite!
Right now, my brother and my sister [3] ....
(*play / do*) tennis. My dad [4] .... (*cook / make*)
sausages and burgers on the barbecue, and my mum and
I … well, we [5] .... (*not do / not work*) anything!
The sun [6] .... (*not light / not shine*), but that's
OK – it's still really hot!
What [7] .... (*you – do / make*) at the moment?

Love,
Lila x

Present simple and continuous

5 Complete the description of the photo. Use the Present simple or Present continuous form of the verbs. Then answer the question below.

This is a photo of my family. ¹ *Do you like* (you/like) it? In this photo, we ² .... (smile) – we ³ .... (smile) a lot in my family. I'm Ángela. I ⁴ .... (sit) in the middle, and my parents (Fran and Gaby) ⁵ .... (stand) behind me. I ⁶ .... (think) my smile is the biggest! In the photo, my dad (Fran) ⁷ .... (wear) a white shirt. He ⁸ .... (usually/wear) T-shirts! My brother Reyes ⁹ .... (appear) on the right, near Mum. Javi is on the left.

Who are the people in the photo? Write the names.

A ....   D ....
B ....   E ....
C ....

Apostrophes

6 Rewrite the text. Add apostrophes where necessary.

My uncle's called Tom. Hes married to Tess, and theyve got six children! My cousin Jakes got five sisters but he hasnt got any brothers. Jakes sisters names are Lily, Gina, Jo, Ava and Meg. Theres also a dog, whos very friendly. Its names Lucky, and it loves long walks when its sunny.

My uncle's called Tom. ....
....
....
....
....
....
....
....

Pronouns and possessive adjectives

7 Complete the sentences with the pronoun or possessive adjective that relates to the words in bold.

1 Is that **Dan**? What's *he* doing here?
2 Please pass this book to **John**. It isn't mine, it's ....
3 They're my **neighbours**. I don't like .... much!
4 **We** live here. This house is ....
5 'What's .... name?' 'It's **Sophie**.'
6 I think **this bag** belongs to **you**. Look, ...'s got .... name on it.

Useful adjectives

8 Complete Evie's holiday journal with these adjectives.

brilliant	colourful	dirty	disgusting	huge
~~lovely~~	popular	quiet	sore	tiny

Saturday

It's a ¹lovely, warm evening in San Francisco. It's a ² .... city – one of the biggest in the USA! It's really ³ .... with tourists, too. I loved the ⁴ .... buildings in blue, green, yellow. My only criticism? My feet feel ⁵ .... after walking all day!

Monday

After the city noise, the Sierra National Forest seems ⁶ .... We're staying in a ⁷ .... village, with just a few houses. The only café is ⁸ .... (it needs a clean!), and the food tastes ⁹ .... ! Dad says we're leaving tomorrow. I think that's a ¹⁰ .... idea.

Comparatives and superlatives

9 Complete the questions. Use the comparative or superlative form of the adjectives. Then answer the questions.

1 Is your best friend *older than* you, or .... you?   (~~old~~/young)
2 Who is .... person in your family? (funny)
3 What is .... place in your country? (beautiful)
4 Do you think films are .... books? (good)
5 What do you think is .... day of the week?   (bad)
6 Is Maths homework .... English homework?   (difficult)

Free-time activities

10 Cross out the word which does *not* belong.

1 do *judo / athletics / ~~the drums~~*
2 listen to *reggae / classical / fantasy* music
3 watch a *horror / rap / comedy* film
4 play *ice hockey / the saxophone / surfing*
5 go *gymnastics / swimming / skiing*

11 Complete the sentences with the Past simple forms of suitable verbs.

On Sunday …

1 Jonah *sent* text messages, ... the drums and .... to rock music.
2 Nell .... basketball, ... gymnastics and .... fantasy films.
3 Ali .... tennis, ... the internet and .... a keyboard.

Relative pronouns

12 Complete the definitions. Write *who*, *which* or *where* and add suitable words.

1 Doctors and nurses are people *who* work in *hospitals*.
2 A teacher is a person .... works in a ....
3 A library is a place .... you can read lots of ....
4 A pen is an object .... you use to .... with.
5 Snakes are long, thin animals .... haven't got any .... !
6 Your .... is the room .... you sleep.
7 Your .... are the people .... you call 'Mum' and 'Dad'.

some and any

13 Write sentences and questions with *some* or *any*. Use the Present simple.

1 I / have got / money with me   ✘
   I haven't got any money with me.
2 There / be / orange juice in the fridge   ✔
   ....
   ....
3 be / there / museums in your town   **?**
   ....
   ....
4 We / have got / lessons / on Saturdays   ✘
   ....
   ....
5 My dad / usually / eats / cereal for breakfast   ✔
   ....
   ....
6 he / like / interesting bands   **?**
   ....
7 I / usually / do / work / on Saturdays   ✘
   ....
   ....

much, many and a lot of

14a Choose the correct options. Then answer the question below.

I've got [1](a lot of / much posters on my bedroom walls. I've got [2]*much / a lot of* sports clothes, but I haven't got [3]*many / much* clean clothes at the moment! I've got quite [4]*a lot of / much* books, but I don't spend [5]*much / many* time reading them! I haven't got [6]*much / many* comics. I like them, but reading comics isn't my favourite hobby. I've got a guitar, but I don't know [7]*many / much* songs yet. I haven't got any drums (my favourite instrument) – Dad says they make too [8]*many / much* noise! Mum says there's too [9]*many / much* mess in my room, but I think it's perfect …

b Compare the picture of Caleb's bedroom with the text. Can you find a mistake in the picture?

Feelings adjectives

15 Put the letters in the correct order to complete feelings adjectives. Which adjectives are positive (☺)?

1 t*ired*   (ider)
2 a...................... (nryg)
3 u...................... (tsep)
4 b...................... (erod)
5 p...................... (odur)
6 lo...................... (lyne)
7 af...................... (idra)
8 ex......................   (itcde)
9 ne......................   (ovurs)
10 je...................... (sloua)
11 re...................... (axeld)
12 em......................   (edbssarar)

Past simple

16 Complete the text. Use the Past simple affirmative, negative or question form of *be.*

I remember a time when I ¹ *was* two. It ² ....
my twin sisters' birthday party. They ³ ....
four that day! There ⁴ .... lots of presents,
but they ⁵ .... for me. I ⁶ ....
very happy. I think I cried! What's your earliest memory?
⁷ .... (it) a happy or a sad time? How old
⁸ .... (you)?

17 Rewrite the sentences and questions in the Past simple.

1 I watch TV and study.
   I watched TV and studied.

2 I don't walk to school.
   ....

3 Do you play the violin? Yes, I do.
   .... ?
   ....

4 He likes Dana, so he carries her books.
   ....

5 Max doesn't talk much because he's shy.
   ....

6 Does Mr Scott live here? No, he doesn't.
   .... ?
   ....

Irregular verbs

18 Complete the text. Use the Past simple form of the verbs.

I ¹ *got* (get) up very late on Saturday. Then I
² .... (eat) a huge breakfast and
³ .... (drink) some coffee. Later,
I ⁴ .... (go) into town and I
⁵ .... (buy) a new video game.
Jamie ⁶ .... (come) round in the
afternoon and we played for a while. He's
really good, so I ⁷ .... (lose)!
After dinner, I ⁸ .... (write) a few
emails and I ⁹ .... (send) some
photos to a friend. Oh, yes, and I
¹⁰ .... (do) a bit of homework,
too! What did you do last Saturday?

Telling the time

19 Write the time in words. Use *to, past* or *o'clock.*

1 **1:45**   *a quarter to two*
2 **9:00**   ....
3 **3:10**   ....
4 **7:45**   ....
5 **3:55**   ....
6 **11:30**   ....

1 Different Lives

Vocabulary Compound nouns

★ **1** Match (1–8) to (a–h) to make compound nouns. Then match them to the pictures.

1 business — a board
2 white — b boat
3 snow — c sitter
4 space — d person *Picture 6*
5 baby — e ship
6 wind — f mill
7 speed — g work
8 home — h mobile

① ② ③ ④ ⑤ ⑥ ⑦ ⑧

★★ **2** Complete the compound nouns in the box. Then use these words to complete the sentences.

| businessp _ _ _ _ n | class _ _ _ e | homew _ _ k |
| skyscr _ _ _ r | ~~speedb o a t~~ | wind _ _ _ l |

1 The world's fastest *speedboat* travelled over the water at a speed of 511 km/h!
2 According to my ...., our Maths teacher is planning a surprise test!
3 I'm sure my English .... is getting easier and easier!
4 I was born in a big .... in the country. Now I live in flat in a tall .... in the city.
5 My mum is a very ambitious person. She's a .... and she wants to start her own company.

★★ **3** Complete the text with compound nouns. Match a word from list A to a word from list B.

| A | ~~class~~ | class | home |
| | light | speed | white |

| B | board | boats | house |
| | mates | ~~room~~ | work |

It's ten o'clock, and I'm sitting in a ¹*classroom* at school. The teacher is writing the answers to last night's ²....................... on the ³....................... . I'm looking out of the window, where I can see the sea. There are some small but fast and noisy ⁴....................... on the water. There's a tall white ⁵....................... on the cliff that warns ships about the dangerous rocks below. It looks like a beautiful day. I wish my ⁶....................... and I could go outside!

★★ **4** Complete the definitions with compound nouns. Use the singular or plural forms.

1 A w*indmill* is a tall building that uses wind power for energy.
2 A c....................... is a person who looks after a building, like a school.
3 S....................... are small vehicles that people use to travel across snow.
4 A s....................... is a vehicle that travels in space.
5 A .... is a tall building that shines a light out to sea to warn ships of dangerous rocks.
6 A .... is a person who looks after children while their parents are out.

Vocabulary page 104

Reading

Brain Trainer

Always read a text at least twice!
Read quickly the first time to
understand the main ideas.
Do not stop reading when you
see difficult words or sentences.
Now do Exercise 1.

★ 1 Read the diary quickly. Complete
the summary with the correct
options.

Sophie is from [1] *the UK / Australia*.
She is writing about her experiences
of [2] *moving to / having a holiday* in
[3] *the UK / Australia*.

★ 2 How do Sophie's feelings about
her experiences change?
Choose the best diagram.

A 😞 → 🙂 → 😞
B 🙂 → 😐 → 😞
C 🙂 → 😞 → 🙂

★★ 3 Read the diary again and find these numbers in the text.
They may appear in a different order. Complete the
sentences.

1 *5* – There are five *classrooms* in the school.
2 *8,000,000* – There are around 8,000,000 ....
in ....
3 *2* – Sophie saw two ....
4 *389* – There are 389 .... in Sophie's
....
5 *45* – .... are forty-five.
6 *15* – There are fifteen .... in the
....

★★ 4 Are the sentences true (T) or false (F)? <u>Underline</u> the
evidence for your answers in the text.

1 Sophie's last home was small.   *F*
2 More people live in Tokyo than London.   ....
3 Sophie isn't pleased when her parents get a
motorbike.   ....
4 All the students at Sophie's new school are friendly.   ....
5 Sophie feels upset about her first day at school.   ....
6 The only way Sophie can get to school is on foot.   ....
7 Sophie walked on an insect by mistake.   ....
8 Sophie still doesn't like everything about her
new home.   ....

A NEW LIFE DOWN UNDER
by SOPHIE HICKS

DAY 1

We came straight from the airport to the farmhouse.
It's *huge*! <u>Our old flat was the opposite of small</u>, but now we
have fifteen rooms, including a sports room with a football
table! Amazing.

DAY 2

This time last week, I was living in one of the world's biggest
cities. More than 8,000,000 people live in London; almost as
many as Tokyo. My new town has got a population of 389!
I miss people, skyscrapers and traffic! We don't even have a
car here.

DAY 4

We've now got a vehicle. But this isn't good news. When
I went outside this morning, Dad and Mum were riding
around the farm on an old motorbike! They were laughing
like teenagers. They're *forty-five*.

DAY 7

There are only five classrooms at my new school (and a
windmill to power the electricity)! I was really nervous at
first, but all my classmates were really nice. Well, apart from
one boy who laughed at my English pronunciation, but I
didn't mind too much. There's always one school idiot!

DAY 10

This morning, Dad offered me a lift to school on the
motorbike, but I was too embarrassed. That was a mistake.
While I was walking, I saw two scorpions and I nearly stood
on a big, black tarantula! In the UK, there were flies and
sometimes a few *little* spiders. Australian insects belong to
horror films!

DAY 15

Maybe this move isn't so bad. Yes, it's quiet, the animals are
scary, and I'm still not sure about the motorbike. But people
are really friendly, and it's hard to be sad when it's sunny
every day!

Grammar Past simple vs Past continuous

★ 1 **Look at the photo. Complete the sentences with the Past simple or Past continuous form of the verbs.**

Past continuous

1 At the time of the crash, Carl *was going* (go) to work.
2 He .... (drink) coffee.
3 He .... (send) a text.
4 He .... (not look) at the road.

Past simple

5 Carl .... (not see) the stop sign.
6 Luckily, he quickly .... (get) better after the accident!
7 He never .... (use) his phone while he was driving again.

★ 2 **Choose the correct options.**

1 A (Did you have) / Were you having a good summer holiday?
   B Lovely, thanks. At this time last week I was on the beach. I *didn't sit / wasn't sitting* in a classroom!
2 A Oh dear! What *happened / was happening* to you?
   B I broke my leg while I *rode / was riding* a snowmobile!
3 A What *did you do / were you doing* when I phoned at nine o'clock last night?
   B Sorry. I *didn't hear / wasn't hearing* the phone. I was doing my homework!

★ 3 **Underline *while* and *when* in the sentences. Complete the sentences with the Past simple or the Past continuous form of the verbs.**

1 While I *was walking* (walk) home one day, I *met* (meet) a man who changed my life.
2 When I .... (be) born, my parents .... (live) in a farmhouse.
3 I .... (lost) my passport while I .... (run) through the airport.
4 I .... (swim) in the sea when I .... (see) Max on a speedboat.
5 Mum and Dad first .... (meet) while they .... (travel) on a steamboat.
6 The light in the lighthouse .... (not work) when the accident .... (happen).

★★ 4 **Complete the text with the Past simple or Past continuous form of the verbs.**

From the streets to the stadium

At this time yesterday, the Brazil women's football team [1] *were playing* (play) in the Homeless World Cup. In the last ten minutes, Luana [2] .... (score) the winning goal! When Luana [3] .... (get) home to her flat afterwards, all her friends [4] .... (wait) for her. There was a big party!

But this time last year, Luana [5] .... (not live) in a flat. She [6] .... (not have) a home at all. While Luana [7] .... (look) for a place to sleep one night, a friend [8] .... (tell) her about the Homeless World Cup. At that time, Brazilian members of the Homeless World Cup charity [9] .... (try) to help homeless people like Luana, by building their confidence through sport.

Luana [10] .... (become) more confident while she [11] .... (learn) new skills. With the charity's help, she [12] .... (win) a scholarship to study at college.

Grammar Reference pages 86–87

Vocabulary Phrasal verbs 1

Brain Trainer

Don't just write lists of new words in your vocabulary notebook. Write example sentences, too, to help you remember how to use the words.

Do Exercise 1. Then write the example sentences for each phrasal verb in your notebook.

★ **1** Match the sentence beginnings (1–8) with the endings (a–h).

1 My dog ran   *d*
2 Could I borrow your pen to fill
3 I'm going on holiday! Would you look
4 Come in and do some work! Don't hang
5 I'll call you after school. When do you usually get
6 We needed extra money, so we set
7 Don't stop trying! Don't give
8 If you don't understand what a word means, find

a in this form?
b back home in the afternoons?
c up just because something's a bit difficult!
d away and we never found her again.
e out by using a dictionary.
f out with your friends doing nothing.
g up our own business.
h after my rabbit while I'm away?

★ **2** Choose the correct options.

1 Please .... your details here.
   a fill in   **b** find out   **c** set up
2 I'm .... my little brother tonight.
   a giving up
   b hanging out
   c looking after
3 They .... a new charity.
   a set up   **b** ran away   **c** filled in
4 I .... that her name was Helen.
   a got back   **b** found out   **c** gave up
5 He .... and now we can't find him!
   a ran away   **b** filled in   **c** set up
6 We .... in town all day.
   a found out   **b** hung out   **c** looked after
7 I can't do this. I .... .
   a give up   **b** get back   **c** run away
8 I missed the last bus, so I .... late.
   a set up   **b** looked after   **c** got back

★ **3** Complete the text with the correct form of these phrasal verbs.

fill in	find out	get back	give up
hang out	~~look after~~	run away	set up

Yesterday was awful! I ¹*was looking after* my little brother while my parents were out. My aunt and uncle ²................................. a new café in town, and my parents went to help them decorate.

I had lots of homework to do. While I ³................................. the answers, Harry got bored. At first, he ⁴................................. in my room. I told him to go away. So he did. He went downstairs, opened the door – and ⁵.................................!

I looked for him everywhere. I didn't ⁶................................. , I kept looking. Eventually, a neighbour phoned, and I ⁷................................. he was playing with a friend! We ⁸................................. home just before my parents did. I didn't tell them!

★ **4** Look at the photos. Use the correct affirmative or negative form of the phrasal verbs from Exercise 3 to complete the sentences.

1 *Please don't hang out* here.

2 ....
this form.

3 ....
my cat.

4 ....
You can do it!

Vocabulary page 104

Chatroom Expressing extremes

Speaking and Listening

★ **1** 🔊 2 **Match the questions (1–6) to the answers (a–f). Then choose the correct options. Listen and check your answers.**

1 So is your new school better than the old one?   *f*
2 What's your favourite subject?
3 Do you do any after-school activities?
4 Do you like your new uniform?
5 What do you think of the school café?
6 Is there anything else you don't like?

a I miss my old friends. They're *so / such* far away!

b It's good! We used to have *so / really* horrible food at my last school!

c No! It's brown. It's *such / so* an ugly colour. It's *such / really* awful!

d I'm in the skateboarding club. It's *so / such* cool!

e English. We've got a *really / such* nice teacher. But I don't like Maths. It's *so / such* a difficult subject!

f I don't think *so* / *really*! But it's different.

★ **2** 🔊 3 **Listen to a conversation. Complete the answers with one word in each gap.**

1 When did Anna move into her new home?
A *month* ago.

2 Did Anna live in a bigger or smaller city before?
A .... city.

3 What's the weather like where Anna is today?
It's ....

4 What can Anna see from her window?
The ....

5 Which person in Anna's family hasn't got a balcony?
Her ....

6 What is Anna sending Jake?
A ....

★★ **3** 🔊 3 **Listen again. What did Anna and Jake say about these things? Complete the sentences with *really*, *so* or *such* and these words or phrases.**

a big city	a mess	a nice
beautiful views	cool house	disappointing
friendly	quiet	sister

1 New Orleans, Louisiana: *It's such a big city.*
2 The small city of Ripon: It's ....
3 Anna's new home: It's a ....
4 The worst thing about Anna's room:
It's ....
5 The best thing about Anna's room:
It's got ....
6 The local people: They're ....
7 The weather: It's ....
8 Anna (according to Jake!):
You're ....

★★ **4** **Choose *one* of the photos below. Imagine you moved to this place last month! Write a conversation with a friend back home. Use *really*, *so* and *such* at least once. Talk about these things, or use your own ideas.**

the people	the place	the weather	your new home

Speaking and Listening page 113

Grammar *used to*

★ 1 **Complete the sentences. Use the affirmative or negative form of *used to*.**

1 This village *used to* be tiny, but then it grew!
2 I .... see fields out of my window. Now I see houses!
3 We .... have much to do here, but now we have a sports centre.
4 My friend Ben .... live here. His family moved here a few years ago.
5 I .... get the bus to school, because there wasn't a bus stop!
6 Sometimes I .... feel a bit bored here, but now I like it a lot.

★ 2 **Complete the questions about life 200 years ago. Use the correct form of *used to* and a verb from the box. Then complete the answers.**

be	have	~~ride~~
travel	visit	work

1 *Did* people *use to ride* snowmobiles?
  No, they didn't.
2 .... people .... on steamboats?
  .... , they did.
3 .... there .... big international airports?
  No, there ....
4 .... children .... in factories?
  Yes, they ....
5 .... schools .... whiteboards?
  No, ... didn't.
6 .... spaceships .... Planet Earth?
  .... , they didn't.
  (We think!)

★★ 3 **Look at the photo. Write sentences about life in London in 1900. Use the correct form of *used to* and these verbs.**

~~be~~	chat	drive
ride	take	wear

1 There / horses in London
  There used to be horses in London.
2 Most men / hats
  ....
  ....
  ....
3 Taxis / down the streets
  ....
  ....
  ....
4 People / on mobile phones
  ....
  ....
  ....
5 Some people / bicycles
  ....
6 Cameras / colour photographs
  ....

★★ 4 **Write questions with the correct form of *used to*. Then answer them so that they're true for you. Use the correct short form.**

Your life aged six

1 you and your family / in a city?   (live)
  Did you and your family use to live in a town?
  Yes, we did./No, we didn't.
2 you / coffee?   (like)
  .... ?
  ....
3 you / to school / by yourself?   (walk)
  .... ?
  ....
4 your best friend / to your school?   (go)
  .... ?
  ....
5 you / cartoons?   (watch)
  .... ?
  ....
6 you and your family / a dog?   (have)
  .... ?
  ....
7 your bedroom / the same colour?   (be)
  .... ?
  ....

▷ **Grammar Reference** pages 86– 87 ▷

Reading

1 Read the article quickly. What is the main purpose of the text? Choose one option.

   a to warn people about road safety
   b to tell an amazing personal story
   c to give a history of the Paralympics
   d to describe wheelchair basketball

LIFESTYLES

The day that changed everything

'The day before yesterday,' says Josh Peters, 16, 'was probably the best day of my life.' On that day, Josh found out that the national basketball team wanted him to play in the Paralympics!

Amazingly, two years ago, Josh didn't use to like any sport. 'I was so lazy,' says Josh. 'The only exercise I did outside school was going to the shops to buy video games!'

On the day before his fourteenth birthday, Josh was crossing the road when a motorbike hit him. The motorcyclist was riding so fast that he didn't see the red light – or Josh. Josh never walked again.

At first, Josh thought his life was over. 'I didn't hang out with friends. I didn't answer their calls or emails. I just wanted to be alone.' Then one day he saw a YouTube video about wheelchair basketball. 'It looked so exciting,' said Josh, 'I wasn't watching "people in wheelchairs". I was watching great athletes!'

Josh joined a wheelchair basketball team in Birmingham. 'My family live in the city now, but we didn't then,' explains Josh, 'so I got a bus from my village every weekend to attend practice sessions. Friends often came with me. I realised how lucky I was to have such great friends.'

Josh wasn't good at wheelchair basketball straightaway. 'I fell over lots, and I felt like such an idiot. I used to play "ordinary" basketball at school, but that's easy. Compared to wheelchair basketball, it's slow!' However, Josh didn't give up, and he quickly impressed his coach, Andy Martin. 'Josh's talent and determination are amazing. He's a Paralympian already.'

How does Josh feel about his accident now? 'Differently. Yes, it changed me. In a good way! Before it happened, I was just an average teenager. Now, I'm competing for my country.'

2 Read the article again. Complete the sentences. Write *one* or *two* words in each gap.

1 Josh had some great news *two* days ago.
2 Two years ago, Josh only used to play .... in his free time.
3 Josh's accident happened when he was .... years old.
4 The accident happened because .... didn't stop at a red light.
5 Josh found out about wheelchair basketball when he watched a ....
6 Two years ago, Josh lived in a ....
7 According to Josh, compared to ordinary basketball, the wheelchair sport is ....
8 Josh mainly feels .... that his life changed.

Listening

1 ◗◗ 4 Listen to a radio programme. What inspired the two main speakers? Choose *one* idea for each person.

a book   a film   a song
a TV programme

1 Rosa: ....
2 Ali: ....

2 ◗◗ 4 Listen again. For each answer, write *Rosa, Ali* or *Rosa and Ali*.

Who …
1 found out what job they wanted to do? *Ali*
2 developed a completely new interest? ....
3 experienced a change on their birthday? ....
4 made a parent unhappy?
5 felt inspired when a friend introduced them to something? ....
6 used to get better marks at school? ....

Writing Telling a story

1 Read the story quickly and put the paragraphs in order.

1 .... 2 .... 3 ....

A birthday surprise

(A) After an amazing dinner and *lots* of cake, Dad set up the stereo in the garden, and we chatted and danced till late. It was a really memorable night. My family and friends are so great. I ¹ *'m* (be) very lucky!

(B) When school finished, I was feeling quite sad. Then, while I ² .... (walk) home, it started to rain. I really ³ .... (not have) a good day! By the time I got home, I just wanted to play video games and forget about everything. So I had such a shock when I ⁴ .... (open) the door – and saw all my family and friends. Everyone was shouting 'surprise'!

(C) I always used to love birthdays, but this year was different. My family ⁵ .... (give) me a few cards at breakfast, and then I went to school. No one in my class remembered it was my birthday. I suggested a cinema trip that night, but everyone said 'sorry, I ⁶ .... (be) busy'.

2 Read the story in Exercise 1 again. Complete the text with the correct form of the verbs. Use the Present simple, Past simple or Past continuous.

3a Complete the sentences. Use the Present simple, Past simple or Past continuous form of these verbs.

know leave live open put ~~walk~~

1 When I *walked* into the classroom, I was feeling really nervous.
2 I .... in the countryside now, but last year I lived in a city skyscraper.
3 Marco .... the ring on Anna's finger when I sneezed! I was so embarrassed.
4 '........................ (you) what time it is?' the new boy asked me.
5 While everyone .... their presents, I took a family photo.
6 When she .... the hospital, she was crying very loudly!

b Match the sentences (1–6) in Exercise 3a to the story headings (a–f) below.

a The first time I met my best friend   4
b My brother's/sister's wedding
c A special family celebration
d My first day at school
e A new baby in the family
f The day we moved house

4 You are going to write a story about a memorable day in your own life. Choose an idea from Exercise 3, or your own ideas. Then make notes in the paragraph plan.

Paragraph 1: the background to the story ....

Paragraph 2: the main event ....

Paragraph 3: conclusion (what happened afterwards and how you felt) ....

5 Write your story. Use the plan from Exercise 4 and include a mix of tenses.

Aiming High

Vocabulary Collocations with *make, go* and *keep*

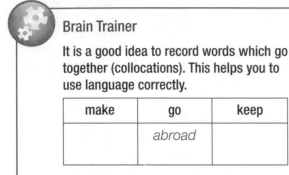

Brain Trainer

It is a good idea to record words which go together (collocations). This helps you to use language correctly.

make	go	keep
	abroad	

Now do Exercise 1.

★ **1** Match the sentence beginnings (1–8) with the endings (a–h).

1 On our last holiday, we went   c
2 She moved to the USA, but we kept
3 I revised every week. It really made
4 It's a nice day. Let's go
5 Relax! Keep
6 Please help me find my cat! She went
7 Yesterday the team made
8 Listen. Can you keep

a calm and try not to worry.
b missing yesterday.
c abroad – to Paris!
d a secret?
e for a walk in the park.
f a difference in my end-of-year exam.
g it to the final.
h in touch by videophone.

★ **2** Choose the correct options.

When I ¹(made)/ went / kept it to the final of the judo competition, it ² made / went / kept my dreams come true. On the day of the final, I was really nervous, so I ³ made / went / kept for a walk. That ⁴ made / went / kept a difference, because it helped me to ⁵ make / go / keep calm. But I didn't take my mobile, so I didn't ⁶ make / go / keep in touch with my mum. That was a mistake. She ⁷ made / went / kept crazy with worry! Luckily, when I returned and won the contest, she forgave me.

★★ **3** Complete the *make, go* and *keep* collocations in the text. Write one word in each gap.

In 2009, an ordinary, 48-year-old woman surprised the world with her beautiful singing on Britain's Got Talent. Fans ¹ *went* crazy when Susan Boyle made ² .... to the final. The judges found it difficult to ³ .... control!

In the final, a dance group won first prize, but fans of the show still made Susan's dreams come ⁴ .... Her first album was number one around the world!

Fame quickly made ⁵ .... big difference to Susan's life. She became very rich, and ⁶ .... abroad to sing in many different countries, including the USA and Australia. But she says she still enjoys 'ordinary' hobbies. She goes ⁷ .... walks, meets friends – and she loves spending time with her cat!

★★ **4** Write the sentences or phrases. Use the correct form of *make, go* or *keep*.

1 *Josh can't keep secrets.* (*Josh / can't / secrets*) He always tells someone.
2 .... (*Mum / crazy*) when I'm late for dinner!
3 .... (*Tom / in touch*) after he moved to the USA.
4 .... (*My parents / a big difference*) to my life when they bought me a laptop.
5 .... (*Marie / always / calm*) when I start worrying.
6 .... (*Our cat / missing*) last year. We later found her in a tree!
7 .... (*My dad / the decision*) to paint the house pink. It wasn't Mum's idea!
8 .... (*We / for a walk*) right now. Are you coming?

Vocabulary page 105

Reading

★ **1** Read the webpage quickly. Then complete the title.

How to m........................
all your d........................
c........................
t........................

★ **2** What kind of writing is the webpage? Choose the correct option.

a a factual report
b an informal article
c a formal essay
d an advertisement

★ **3** Read the webpage again. Match the headings (a–f) to the gaps (1–5). There is one heading you do not need.

a Learn to love your mistakes
b Work hard
c How I can help you
d How to get rich
e Be yourself
f Have clear aims

★ **4a** Read the statements (1–7). According to the writer of the webpage are the statements true (T), false (F) or don't know (DK)?

1 Everyone has dreams for the future.   *T*
2 Achieving your dreams can be difficult.   ....
3 It's best to start with a large, general aim.   ....
4 Life is easy when you're famous.   ....
5 Successful people don't make mistakes.   ....
6 Happiness is the most important thing in life.   ....
7 Being successful means being rich.   ....

b Look at the statements in Exercise 3b again. What do you think?

---

www.yourlifenow.org

HOME   NEWS   GUIDES   FEATURES   PHOTOS

....

1 ....

Have you ever had any dreams for the future? Yes, of course you have! But making your dreams come true isn't always easy. For the last ten years I've studied the lives of successful men and women, and my research has changed my life. But I don't want to keep my discoveries secret. Now let me share my best ideas with YOU!

2 ....

Lots of people think 'I want to be rich/successful/famous', but these aims aren't helpful. They're too big! Instead, make a decision about exactly what you want to achieve in life and why. For example: 'I've always loved writing. I want to study literature at university and then find work in the media.'

3 ....

Have you ever noticed how busy celebrities are? Yes, they go to lots of parties, but they don't often sit down and relax. They're always planning their next book, or film, or media interview. In reality, very few successful people are lazy. Sorry about that!

4 .*a*.

If you've never failed in life, you aren't human! If you get a bad mark, lose a competition or argue with your friends, keep calm. Think about what's just happened. Can you do anything differently the next time? Failure is an excellent teacher.

5 ....

Finally, your biggest aim is to be happy! It's a good idea to listen to advice from parents or teachers, but remember that it's your life, and your dreams. What does 'success' mean to you? Does it mean having lots of money, or being close to family and friends? You decide.

HOW TO GUIDE NO. 58
Do You have a dream?

Grammar Present perfect

★ **1** Choose the correct options.

1 We've *already* / *ever* / *yet* entered the contest.

2 Has the team *ever* / *just* / *already* made it to the final before? No. This is their first time!

3 Why are you smiling? I've *already* / *yet* / *just* heard some amazing news.

4 I've *yet* / *ever* / *never* won any competitions before. This is a new experience for me.

5 Have you done your homework *just* / *ever* / *yet*? Yes. I've finished it!

6 She's *never* / *already* / *yet* made it to the finals. She's very talented.

7 I've *ever* / *yet* / *never* been on a motorbike. It looks dangerous!

8 I haven't been to the USA *yet* / *already* / *just*, but I'd like to go there one day.

★ **2** Complete the sentences with *for* or *since*. (Which sentences are true for you?)

1 I haven't eaten anything *since* breakfast.

2 I've studied English .... more than ten years.

3 I've known my best friend .... primary school.

4 I haven't listened to any music .... I got up.

5 I've lived in the same place .... my whole life.

6 I've had my own bedroom .... I was little.

7 I haven't watched any TV .... last night.

8 I haven't been to the cinema .... more than a month.

★★ **3** Complete the text with these words. Then answer the question below.

already	~~ever~~	for	just	never	since	yet

Woodford School's basketball team has won the finals! Maisie is organising a party to celebrate.

Have you ¹ ever organised a party before? Who did you invite?

• Maisie has invited Jez, but she hasn't talked to Layla ² ....

• Ellie hasn't kept in touch with anyone ³ .... she moved house.

• Matt has ⁴ .... been to a school party before, so he was excited to get an invitation.

• Jake has ⁵ .... received an invitation by text. Matt sent it two seconds ago!

• No one has seen Hasan ⁶ .... a week. He's been on holiday with his parents.

• Ed has ⁷ .... arranged to meet Layla at the party. He phoned her a while ago.

Who doesn't know about the party yet? .... and ....

★★ **4** Complete the conversations. Use the Present perfect with *already, ever, just, never* or *yet*.

1 **A** Why are they so happy?

B I think *their favourite team has just won*! (their favourite team / win)

2 **A** Have you ever visited New York?

B No. ....

.... !

I prefer holidays at home. (I / go abroad)

3 **A** Do you want to watch *Avatar*?

B No, thanks. ....

....

We saw it a few years ago. (we / see / it)

4 **A** Please can I go out?

B No, sorry! ....

.... !

(you / not finish / dinner)

5 **A** I haven't heard from Tess for ages. How's she doing?

B Actually, ...

....

Read this! (she / text / me)

6 **A** I can't decide where to go on holiday this year.

B ....

to Spain? It's my favourite country. (you / go)

Grammar Reference pages 88–89

Vocabulary Jobs and suffixes -or, -er, -ist

★ **1** Complete the table with the jobs. Write the letters in the correct order.

artform or object	person (job)
building	¹ *builder* (ldiurbe)
poem	² .... (tpeo)
novel	³ .... (nliovets)
play	⁴ .... (wrayhtplig)
art	⁵ .... (ratsit)
sculpture	⁶ .... (ostulprc)
photo	⁷ .... (grpotohhreap)

★ **2** Complete the words in these definitions. Decide if it is a word for a *thing* or a *person*.

1 An art*ist* paints or draws.
2 A doct.......... helps sick people.
3 A poe.......... is a short piece of writing. It may use special, beautiful language.
4 A novel.......... writes books with stories.
5 A build.......... makes things like houses, flats and walls.
6 A sculpt.......... is a kind of art that people make, for example, with metal, wood or stone.
7 A dent.......... helps us to have healthy teeth.
8 A play.......... writes stories for the theatre.

★ **3** Complete the culture facts with the correct form of these words. There is one word you don't need.

art   build   novel   photo   play   poem   ~~sculpture~~

1 Antony Gormley is a British *sculptor*. His famous metal *Angel of the North* is 20 metres tall and 54 metres wide!
2 The .... Dante Alighieri was born in Florence, Italy. People have translated his poems into hundreds of languages.
3 Pablo Picasso was a famous Spanish .... He started painting when he was a child!
4 Shakespeare loved the theatre. He was a .... and an actor. He also wrote poems.
5 The American .... Christopher Paolini started writing his first book, *Eragon*, aged fifteen!
6 The Great Wall of China is the longest wall in the world. It had millions of .... !

★★ **4** Complete the adverts. Write a job or an art word in each gap.

① **Do you want beautiful, white teeth?**
At *WhiteSmile* you can find all the best *dentists* in town.

② *Today's World* is looking for a new .... to take pictures for the newspaper. Can you take interesting, beautiful .... ? Send us some examples.

③ **Are you a** .... ?
Send *TruePoetry* a .... on the topic of 'love.' Write no more than 50–100 words. There's a prize for the best one.

④ Come to the **SWAN THEATRE** tonight to see Shakespeare's most famous .... about love, **ROMEO AND JULIET.**

⑤ • Do you need a .... ?
• Walls, rooms, roofs – you name it, Bob can build it!
• Call for details.

⑥ **Have you got a cold?**
You don't need to see a .... or a nurse! You can buy **ColdAway** medicine for just £4.99.

Chatroom Giving/Responding to news

Speaking and Listening

★ **1** Read Harry's news. Tick (✓) the three correct responses.

> I've just made it to the finals of *Pop Idol*!

Harry

Harry's friends:
1 I swear it's true!
2 No way!
3 You won't believe it!
4 Unbelievable!
5 I'm hopeless!
6 You're kidding me!
7 Seriously.
8 What's up?

★ **2** 🔊 **5** Complete the conversation with these words and phrases. Then listen and check.

believe	kidding	Seriously
~~the most amazing~~	true	Unbelievable
up	way	

Orla Who was that on the phone? And why are you smiling?
Luke Oh, it was my dad. I've just heard ¹*the most amazing* piece of news.
Orla What's ²...................?
Luke Well, you know I entered that nature photography competition?
Orla Yes, you sent in a photo of a blackbird, I remember.
Luke Well, you won't ³................... it, but I've won!
Orla No ⁴...................!
Luke ⁵.................... I swear it's ⁶.................... And the first prize is a holiday to Italy!
Orla ⁷...................! You're so lucky. But it was a great photo. I'm hopeless at photography!
Luke Hey, do you want to come? The prize is for four people, and Mum and Dad say I can bring a friend.
Orla Really? You're ⁸................... me. That would be amazing!

Speaking and Listening page 114

> **Brain Trainer**
>
> Listen to conversations in your Workbook and repeat them to improve your speaking skills.
>
> Listen to recording 5 again and notice how the speakers emphasise words to show interest. Now read the conversation in Exercise 2 out loud, copying the intonation.

★★ **3** 🔊 **6** Listen to a conversation. Then correct the mistakes in these sentences.
1 The conversation is between ~~two~~ *three* friends.
2 Zeke throws a basketball .... to Alice.
3 Zeke has written an article ....
4 He wrote it when he was in a café ....
5 Zeke's work is on page seventeen ....
6 It's about a missing child ....

★★ **4** 🔊 **6** Complete these extracts from the conversation. Write one or two words in each gap. Listen again and check.

A
Zeke I've ¹*just heard* the most amazing piece of news.
Tom So, come on then, ²...................... story?
Alice Yeah, what's ³...................... ?
B
Zeke It's the 'story of the week'!
Alice ⁴...................... way!
Tom You're ⁵...................... .
Zeke Seriously. I ⁶...................... true.

★★ **5** Choose *one* of the situations in the pictures. Imagine that this event has just happened to you. Write a conversation with a friend, giving your news. Use expressions from Exercises 1, 2 and 4.

Grammar Present perfect vs Past simple

★ **1** We can complete sentences A and B in different ways. Match the sentence endings (1–6) to A or B.

A I've lived here …
B We moved here …

1 .A.. all my life.
2 .... last summer.
3 .... in August.
4 .... for three years.
5 .... yesterday.
6 .... since 2000.

★ **2** Choose the correct options in the news article.

It's October 2011, and Fauja Singh ¹*has just finished* / *finished* the Toronto Waterfront Marathon. He ²*has started* / *started* the marathon eight hours, twenty-five minutes and seventeen seconds ago!

Many people ³*have already run* / *already ran* much faster marathons. In April 2011, Geoffrey Mutai of Kenya ⁴*has completed* / *completed* the Boston marathon in two hours, three minutes and two seconds!

But on the day of the Toronto marathon, Fauja ⁵*amazed* / *has amazed* the world. Why? Well, no one ⁶*has ever completed* / *completed* a marathon at the age of 100 before!

Fauja ⁷*has lived* / *lived* in the UK since 1992, but he ⁸*was* / *has been* born in India – in 1911. He announced his retirement in 2013.

Grammar Reference pages 88– 89

★★ **3** Complete the Amazing Facts. Use the Present perfect or the Past simple form of these verbs.

collect	complete	ever/wear	go
grow	~~love~~	put	take

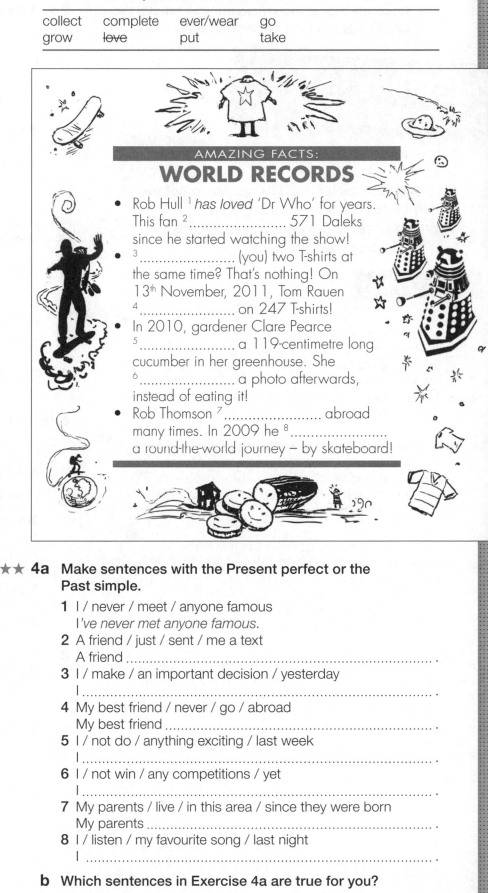

AMAZING FACTS:
WORLD RECORDS

- Rob Hull ¹*has loved* 'Dr Who' for years. This fan ²....................... 571 Daleks since he started watching the show!
- ³....................... (you) two T-shirts at the same time? That's nothing! On 13ᵗʰ November, 2011, Tom Rauen ⁴....................... on 247 T-shirts!
- In 2010, gardener Clare Pearce ⁵....................... a 119-centimetre long cucumber in her greenhouse. She ⁶....................... a photo afterwards, instead of eating it!
- Rob Thomson ⁷....................... abroad many times. In 2009 he ⁸....................... a round-the-world journey – by skateboard!

★★ **4a** Make sentences with the Present perfect or the Past simple.

1 I / never / meet / anyone famous
   I*'ve never met anyone famous*.
2 A friend / just / sent / me a text
   A friend ....
3 I / make / an important decision / yesterday
   I ....
4 My best friend / never / go / abroad
   My best friend ....
5 I / not do / anything exciting / last week
   I ....
6 I / not win / any competitions / yet
   I ....
7 My parents / live / in this area / since they were born
   My parents ....
8 I / listen / my favourite song / last night
   I ....

b Which sentences in Exercise 4a are true for you?

Reading

1 Read the magazine article quickly. What's the oldest age people can send ideas?

50 things to do before you're 18!

If you haven't turned eighteen yet, *MyWorld* magazine wants to hear from you! We want your suggestions for a **'50 things to do before you're 18' list**. Begin with the question **'Have you ever … ?'** We only want ideas you've already tried yourself!

Your replies

1 .c. I've been amazed how quickly I've improved! It's really satisfying. I've been in my own band a year now, and we've even won a few competitions! I've made loads of friends that way, too. Everyone you meet likes music, so you've already got lots to talk about. – *Kitty, Hull*

2 .... Well, why not? Bad weather makes us sad, but this is a way to feel happy again. Yes, you do need to feel confident to try this! Some people have laughed at me, it's true – but many more have joined in! – *Ben, Penrith*

3 .... I can't believe there are people out there who've never seen the sun come up! You don't need to be a poet or an artist to find that beautiful. Oh, and this is an extra idea, but go swimming with dolphins! I did it last summer and now I can't stop telling everyone how amazing it was. – *Lucy, Aberdeen*

4 .... Yesterday I helped to look for a man's dog. The day before that, I stood up when an old lady got on the bus, and I gave her my seat. These people weren't friends or family. They were simply people who needed help. And helping them made me feel great. Try it! It's quite surprising. – *Prash, Nottingham*

5 .... I've tried red, gothic black – and blue! I did it in the school holidays, so teachers didn't complain. (Warning: check that your parents are cool with this first! You don't want them to go crazy.) Or experiment with different clothes instead. It's great fun. There's lots of time to look 'serious' when you're an adult! – *Faith, Preston*

2a Write questions. Begin with *Have you ever …* .

a dance / in the rain?
....?

b change / the colour of your hair?
....?

c learn / how to play a musical instrument?
....?

d stay / up all night?
....?

e do / something nice for someone you don't know?
....?

b Read the replies from *MyWorld* readers. Match the questions (a–e) to the emails (1–5).

3 What is similar about these suggestions?
They're all ways to:
a be very successful
b feel good or happy
c impress your family or friends

4 Which idea do you like best?

Listening

1 🔊 7 Listen to the writer of one of the emails in Reading Exercise 1. Write the correct name.

2 🔊 7 Listen again. Tick (✓) the things the speaker has done.

1 been abroad
2 spoken to a celebrity
3 been on a scary ride
4 been to a sports event
5 ridden a motorbike
6 swum with sharks

3 Look at the adverts. Which holiday activity do you think the speaker would be most interested in?

a **See the sights of Rome on a photography tour** ....

b **Learn a new language at our summer camp!** ....

c **See the white tigers at Whitchurch Zoo** ....

Writing A biography

1 Read the biography quickly. How does Martha know her 'hero'?

Martha is Ewa's ....

Inspirations and Heroes: we celebrate the people who've inspired you!

My hero: Ewa Jarvis (Babcia) **by Martha Jarvis**

Ewa Babcia was born in Poland **in 1945**. She wanted to study cooking at college, but her family were poor, so **when** she was sixteen she started work in a factory. She hated it! She dreamt about baking.

Luckily, **a year later**, Ewa met my grandfather, Reggie, a British photographer. He loved her cooking! **The following year** they got married and moved to London.

At that time, Ewa only spoke Polish. **During the day** she worked in a café, and at night she studied. **After two years**, her English was excellent! **In 1971** my dad was born, and Ewa opened a bakery.

The bakery has been a big success. **A few years ago**, Ewa even made it to the finals of a TV cooking show! **Today**, she's writing her own recipe book.

My gran is my hero because she's made her dreams come true, and she's never given up. (Also, no one's ever made better apple cake ☺.)

2 Read the biography again. Put these events in order. Use the time expressions in bold in the biography to help you.

a she did well in a cookery competition ....
b she started writing a book ....
c she met her future husband ....
d she got a job in a café ....
e she moved to the UK ....
f she got a job in a factory *1.*
g she started her own business ....
h she spoke English really well for the first time ....

3 Complete the sentences. Use some of the words in bold from the biography in Exercise 1.

My hero, Matt Groening, was born in the USA [1] in 1954. Like Bart Simpson, he didn't use to like school [2] .... he was young!

[3] .... 1972 he went to Evergreen State College. [4] .... his time at college, he decided to be a writer and artist. Five years [5] ...., he left Evergreen. [6] .... several months of doing terrible jobs (including cleaning tables!), he felt very tired, but he didn't give up. [7] .... the following year he sold his first cartoon!

I watched my first Simpsons cartoon ten years [8] .... Since then, I've wanted to be a cartoonist, too!

4 You are going to write a biography of your hero for the *Heroes and Inspirations* website. Choose a person who's inspired you. Then make notes about their life.

Name ....
Born ....
Education/Family ....
....
Work ....
....
Other achievements ....
....
How/inspire/you ....
....

5 Write your biography. Use your notes from Exercise 4 and include at least four different time expressions.

....
....
....
....
....
....
....
....

3 Be Happy!

Vocabulary Showing feelings

★ **1** Match the verbs (1–8) to the feelings (a–h).

1 cry
2 smile
3 frown
4 blush
5 sweat
6 gasp
7 yawn
8 shiver

a hot
b surprised
c tired
d upset
e cold
f embarrassed
g in a bad mood
h happy

★ **2** Choose the correct options.

1 I once *smiled /* ⟨*screamed*⟩ loudly during a frightening film.

2 I sometimes *shout / cry* when I read a sad book.

3 When my teacher gave me this homework, I *blushed / sighed*.

4 I never *frown / laugh* when someone falls over. It isn't funny!

5 I rarely *gasp / shout* when I'm angry. I'm usually quite quiet.

6 Sometimes I *yawn / gasp* when I'm tired.

★ **3** Choose the correct options.

1 She cried when she failed her exams, because she was .... .
a angry ⟨b⟩ upset c happy

2 Everyone laughed when I fell over. I felt .... and blushed!
a fed up b cold c embarrassed

3 I was really .... when I won the lottery! I didn't believe it.
a fed up b frightened c surprised

4 Tom was .... , so he went to bed early.
a angry b tired c embarrassed

5 Ella is .... because we forgot her birthday. I feel terrible!
a happy b amused c in a bad mood

6 It's rained all day! I'm bored and .... .
a fed up b hot c amused

Vocabulary page 106

★★ **4** What's happening and why? Write sentences using the correct form of a verb from A and an adjective from B. There are two words in each list you don't need.

A			
~~cry~~	frown	laugh	scream
shiver	sigh	sweat	yawn

B			
amused	bad	cold	embarrassed
frightened	hot	tired	~~upset~~

1 He's *crying because he's upset.*
2 She ....
3 He ....
4 They ....
5 She ....
6 He ....

Reading

★ **1** Read the article quickly. Which description best describes the writer's general attitude to 'colour psychology'?

   a It sounds interesting.   **b** I don't believe it!

★ **2** Read the article again. What does the writer say that the colours mean? Match (1–6) to (a–f).

1 green	**a** money
2 red	**b** power
3 purple	**c** energy
4 blue	**d** intelligence
5 orange	**e** relaxation
6 black	**f** feelings

★ **3** Read the text again and correct the sentences. Tick (✓) the sentence which is correct.

1 Green is a popular colour in hospitals and ~~fast food restaurants~~.
Green is a popular colour in hospitals and cafés.

2 It's a good idea to wear red for arguments.

....

3 The writer's bedroom used to be white.

....

4 'I'm feeling blue' means 'I'm really happy'.

....

5 The writer likes orange clothes.

....

6 Lawyers wear black because they want to look thin.

....

> ### Brain Trainer
>
> When you read a word or expression you don't know, read the text carefully for clues about the meaning. Can you think of another word or expression which would fit the context?
>
> Now do Exercise 4.

★ **4** Find these words and expressions in the article. Choose the best definition.

1 power (introduction) – (ability) / rule / emotion

2 be in trouble (red) – *be happy / have problems / be in danger*

3 symbolises (purple) – *looks / shows / means*

4 be careful (blue) – *think so you don't make a mistake / be free and happy / keep calm*

5 booster (orange) – *something that makes something worse / happier / better*

6 look like (black) – *appear similar to / like a lot / look very closely at*

Feeling blue?

by Carlos Martinez, psychologist

According to 'colour psychology', colours have the power to influence our feelings – and even our lives.

green
Some people believe this is the colour of health. I'm not sure about that, but certainly this calm, relaxing colour is more popular in hospitals than sports stadiums! You often see green paint in cafés, too, but not in many fast food restaurants. They want you to leave quickly!

red
Red is a strong, energetic colour. Wear it when you want to feel confident – for example, on a romantic date. Don't wear it if you're in trouble with a parent or teacher. Angry people are more likely to shout if they see red!

purple
Hundreds of years ago, purple clothes were very expensive. Today, the colour still symbolises wealth. Chinese Feng Shui experts believe that having purple in your home can make you rich, while red can bring good fortune. I've just painted my boringly white bedroom in both colours. Wish me luck!

blue
Blue is popular with artists, because it is the colour of emotions. However, be careful. We don't say 'I'm feeling blue' when we're laughing and smiling, but when we're fed up.

orange
A friend told me that orange is a brain 'booster'! I didn't believe her at first, but I tried it anyway. I look terrible in orange, so I put lots of orange things on my desk instead. I think it helped! I felt happier, and I remembered more.

black
Celebrities like black, because it makes people look thinner! But it's also popular with people in authority, like lawyers and businesspeople. That's because wearing black also helps you to look strong and important. But *smile*. You don't want to look like Dracula!

Grammar Gerunds and infinitives

★ 1 **Complete the table with the examples.**

Dancing makes me happy.	~~I love swimming.~~
I'm happy to cook.	I'm keen on singing.
I want to learn the guitar.	I watch TV to relax.

Use a gerund (-*ing* form):
after certain verbs [1] *I love swimming.*
after prepositions [2] ....
as the subject or object of a sentence [3] ....
Use an infinitive:
after certain verbs [4] ....
after certain adjectives [5] ....
to explain purpose [6] ....

★ **2a** **Rania texts her friends the question 'How are you?' Complete their replies.**

1 Not so good. I hate *to do /* (*doing*) homework!

2 Good! It was lovely *to see / seeing* you last night. x

3 I'm fed up with *to stay / staying* in. I'm so bored!

4 Tired! I want *to go / going* to bed, but it's only 9 p.m.!

5 Tired! But *to run / running* was great. I managed 7 km!

6 Bad day. I'm eating chocolate *to feel / feeling* better!

b **Read the texts again and answer the question.**

How many people are feeling positive? ☺

....

★★ **3** **Complete the text. Use the correct gerund or infinitive form of the verbs.**

How to make friends and influence people!

1 Try *to sound* (sound) positive. Most of us prefer .... (spend) time with happy people!

2 Start a conversation by .... (ask) questions.

3 It's very important .... (listen), too.

4 .... (lie) is a bad idea. Be honest!

5 Look into someone's eyes .... (show) interest.

6 Remember .... (smile)!

★★ **4** **Complete the sentences (1–6). Then match them to the situations (A–F).**

~~cry~~	feel	go	lie	play	shout

1 Cheer up. *Crying* doesn't help.   C

2 I hate .... Please calm down!   ....

3 It's too cold! I don't want .... this game any more.   ....

4 I'm scared of .... to the dentist. It hurts!   ....

5 This is relaxing! I'd be quite happy .... here all morning.   ....

6 When I'm sad I sometimes eat junk food .... better.   ....

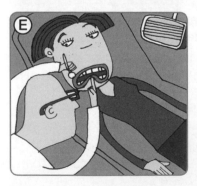

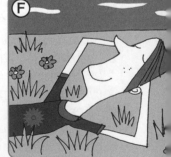

Grammar Reference pages 90–91

Vocabulary Adjective suffixes

★ **1a** Complete the table with the adjectives.

noun + suffix (*-ful*, *-ous* or *-y*) → adjective	
health	[1] *healthy*
luck	[2] ....
wealth	[3] ....
danger	[4] ....
fame	[5] ....
poison	[6] ....
peace	[7] ....
success	[8] ....
beauty	[9] ....

b Which two adjectives have a mainly negative meaning?

.... and ....

★ **2** Choose the correct options.

1 I'm not interested in being *fame /(famous)*.

2 Stop! Don't drink that *poison / poisonous*!

3 It's important to take care of your *health / healthy*.

4 I dream of being *wealth / wealthy* one day.

5 You need lots of *luck / lucky* to be famous.

6 I live in a small, *peace / peaceful* village.

★ **3a** Complete the life advice with the adjective form of the nouns. Use the suffixes *-ful*, *-ous* and *-y*.

1 ❝ It's better to be happy than to be *wealthy* (wealth). ❞

2 ❝ .... (success) people believe in themselves. ❞

3 ❝ Being .... (beauty) is less important than being nice. ❞

4 ❝ If you're happy and .... (health), you're rich. ❞

5 ❝ Having too much money can be .... (danger). ❞

6 ❝ If you want to be .... (fame), you need to work hard, have lots of talent – and be very, very, ... (luck). ❞

b Which piece of advice do you like best?

★★ **4** Complete the star sign personality profiles with the adjective form of the nouns.

beauty	danger	~~fame~~	health
luck	peace	success	wealth

Aries , Leo , Sagittarius

People with these star signs love attention! They dream of being [1] *famous*, like celebrities. They like exciting, [2] .... hobbies, like surfing and climbing. They rarely feel frightened!

Gemini , Libra , Aquarius

People with these star signs are often very [3] .... people – bad luck rarely comes their way! They are usually quite [4] .... , because they enjoy exercise and good food.

Cancer , Scorpio , Pisces

People with these star signs are often [5] .... , quiet people. They don't like shouting! They like looking at [6] .... things, like paintings, or enjoying music and poetry.

Taurus , Virgo , Capricorn

People with these star signs are often very [7] .... at school and work because they try hard to make their dreams come true. They're often [8] .... because they're good with money.

★★ **5a** Complete the people's dreams with the correct noun or adjective form of these words. There are two words you don't need.

beauty	health	luck	~~fame~~
peace	poison	success	wealth

1 Zak: I dream about *fame*. I want to be a celebrity!

2 Ana: I want to help protect the environment from .... chemicals.

3 Tim: I want to end war and fighting, and help create .... on earth.

4 Tillie: I hope I become .... so that I can buy lots of nice things!

5 Hasan: I want to be .... , like my parents. My dad's a doctor and my mum's a famous playwright.

6 Jo: I want to win the lottery. Wish me .... !

b Write your own dream.

Chatroom Invitations

Speaking and Listening

★ 1 Complete the table with these words and expressions.

~~fancy~~   like   I'd   I'll   I'm   I'm going   want

Inviting
Do you ¹ *fancy* + *-ing*?
Do you ² .... to … ?
Would you ³ .... to … ?

Accepting
That's a great idea. ⁴ .... love to.
OK, thanks. ⁵ .... see you there.

Rejecting
That sounds fun, but I can't, ⁶ .... afraid.
Sorry. ⁷ .... to have to say no.

★ 2 🔊 8 Complete the phone conversation with the correct options. Then listen and check.

Ali Hi, Rosa, it's Ali. Do you ¹(*fancy*)/ *want* going bowling tonight?

Rosa Hi, Ali! That sounds fun, but ² *I can't / I'd love to*, I'm afraid. I'm doing homework tonight.

Ali Really? Oh, OK.

Rosa ³ *Would you like to / Do you fancy* see the new Pixar film at the cinema?

Ali That's a great idea. ⁴ *I'd love to / I'm afraid*. Do you ⁵ *want / fancy* going on Saturday?

Rosa Sorry. ⁶ *I'm going to have to / I'd love to* say no. It's my dad's birthday that night. Do you ⁷ *like / want* to go tonight, at 7.30?

Ali OK, thanks. ⁸ *I'll / I'd* see you there. Hey, wait! Aren't you doing homework tonight?

Rosa Oh, yes. But only for a short time. Sorry, Ali. The truth is, I really hate bowling!

Speaking and Listening page 115

★★ 3 🔊 9 Listen to a phone conversation. Then answer the questions.

1 What does Bella want to play with Nick? *basketball*

2 What has Nick hurt? ....

3 How old is Nick's sister? ....

4 What are Bella and Nick going to eat tonight? ....

5 What *doesn't* Bella like? ....

6 What time are Bella and Nick meeting? ....

★★ 4a 🔊 9 Listen again. Number the sentences in the order you hear them.

a That's a great idea. I'd love to. ....
....

b OK, thanks. I'll see you then. ....
....

c Do you fancy watching a film? ....
....

d Do you want to play basketball this afternoon? .1. ....*inviting*.......

e Sorry, but I'm going to have to say no. ....
....

f That sounds fun, but I can't, I'm afraid. ....
....

g Would you like to hang out later? ....
....

b For each sentence, write *inviting*, *accepting*, or *rejecting*.

★★ 5 Write a conversation with a friend. Use the ideas below and phrases from Exercises 1–4.

- invite your friend to do something fun this weekend. (What? When?)

- your friend can't go. (Why not?)

- invite your friend to do another activity at a different time.

- your friend can go!

Possible activities (or use your own ideas!)

go cycling

go shopping

go for a walk

play video games

go swimming

Grammar Present perfect continuous

★ **1** **Match (1–6) with (a–f) to make short conversations.**

1 You look tired.   *e*
2 Why are you shivering?
3 Why are you laughing?
4 Why are you so angry with me?
5 You're sweating!
6 You look surprised.

a Oh, Luna's been telling us jokes for the last half hour!
b Why? I've been waiting for you for ages!
c I've been standing in the cold for an hour!
d Yes. Your teacher has been telling us what a good student you are!
e Yes. We've been working all evening.
f Are we? Sorry! Jo's been playing tennis with me.

★ **2** **Complete the sentences with the Present perfect continuous form of the verbs. Why is the joke in question 1 funny?**

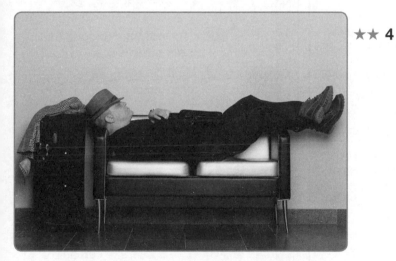

1 *Have you been waiting* (you/wait) long?
2 I'm fed up. It .... (rain) all day.
3 She's really happy with her exam results. She .... (smile) all afternoon!
4 I can't sleep! My neighbours .... (play) loud music for ages.
5 I'm really tired. I .... (not sleep) well all week!
6 Mr Green is in a bad mood. He .... (frown) all lesson.
7 I don't think she's enjoying my poem. She .... (yawn) since I started reading it!
8 Why are you shivering? What .... (you/do)?

★★ **3** **Phoebe's been having a party! But there's a problem. Read what she says, then complete the guests' replies. Use the Present perfect continuous form of these verbs.**

blush	chat	dance	~~play~~	sit	tidy	watch

Phoebe I'm really angry. Someone's just broken my mum's favourite vase. Who did it?

Beth It wasn't me! ¹ *I've been playing* computer games all night.

Mark It wasn't me! I ² .... in this chair for hours.

Layla Maybe it was Dan? He ³ .... to music all night!

Tom It wasn't Josie. She ⁴ .... up in the kitchen all evening.

Olivia Don't look at me! I ⁵ .... to Tom for the last half hour. We haven't moved!

Arthur Maybe it was your brother? I ⁶ .... him since you asked your question. He ⁷ .... red the whole time!

★★ **4** **What's been happening? Read the conversations. Complete the replies. Use the Present perfect continuous form of suitable verbs.**

1 A You all look very fed up!
   B We are! We*'ve been doing* homework for hours!
2 A Why has your dad got paint all over his clothes?
   B He .... my bedroom. Do you want to have a look?
3 A Why are my books all over the floor?
   B Sorry. We .... them.
4 A You look very hot!
   B Yes. I .... aerobics. I don't think I'm very fit!
5 A What's that noise?
   B It's my sister. She .... awful rock music all afternoon.
6 A Why is the kitchen in such a mess?
   B Sorry! I .... a cake for Ella's birthday. I'll tidy up!
7 A Why is his hair wet?
   B He .... in the pool.

Grammar Reference pages 90– 91

Reading

1 Read the web article quickly. Match the jobs to the photos. There is one photo you don't need.

Unusual jobs

← → C ⌂

| HOME | NEWS | FEATURES | PHOTOS | COMMENTS |

Unusual jobs part 9: Jobs that make people laugh!

A ▷▷ I've been working as a professional clown for nearly two years. Before that, I was a comedian for nine years. I was never famous, but I was quite successful! I changed jobs because I wanted to do more in life than make people laugh. What if I could help people, too?

As a clown, I try to encourage sick children in hospital to laugh and smile. When you laugh, your mind and body relax. Apparently, people who laugh more don't suffer from as many colds or other problems! Children who laugh a lot often get better results in their studies, too.

It isn't an easy job. Not all sick children get better, and sometimes I come home and cry. But I always go back to work the next day with my red nose on. I don't earn much money as a clown, but I feel very lucky to work with such brave, wonderful patients.

B ▷▷ I became a laughter yoga teacher more than two years ago. I was originally a dentist! My old job was very difficult, and I used to feel fed up. Now I still improve people's health, but everything else is completely different. Everyone has fun in a laughter yoga class, including the teacher!

No, laughter isn't 'magic'. It doesn't prevent all illnesses, keep you young, or make you beautiful. But did you know that it's an excellent kind of exercise? You move your whole body when you laugh!

Sometimes I work with famous celebrities. It's true that being rich can be stressful! Some famous people can be unpleasant at times, but I try to change their bad moods. Laughter is excellent for people like musicians, artists and writers, because it helps people to be more creative.

2 Read the article again. Answer the questions. Write *A*, *B*, *both* or *neither*.

Who:
1 has done their job for two years?   *B*
2 has been making people laugh for more than ten years?
3 has been famous?
4 has a job connected to health?
5 sometimes feels sad at work?
6 doesn't always like the people they work with?

3 According to the texts in Exercise 1, what are the benefits of laughter? Tick (✓) five ideas.

1 more happiness
2 better study skills
3 more beautiful appearance
4 less stress
5 more fitness
6 no illnesses
7 more artistic ability
8 more wealth

Listening

1 ◗◗ 10 ◀ Listen to a radio programme. Complete the tip sheet heading.

> **Tips** for times when you
> .... !
>
> **1** The best time to go to bed is *ten o'clock*.
> **2** Most people need to sleep for around .... to .... hours a night.
> **3** When you're tired, drink ....
> **4** Exercise in the .... or in the ....
> **5** Eating dark .... can help.
> **6** Do something you enjoy, like ....

2 ◗◗ 10 ◀ Listen again. Complete the tips. Can you add any more ideas?

Writing A 'for and against' essay

1 Read the title of the essay in Exercise 2. Then read the student notes. Are these arguments for or against the topic?

1 more people to talk to? for
2 smaller number of very good friends – more important? ....
3 making friends online can be dangerous? ....
4 don't need to feel bored – always someone to chat to? ....
5 not healthy to spend more time socialising on internet than in real life? ....

2 Read the essay. Which idea in Exercise 1 is not used?

Having lots of friends on social networking sites is important for happiness.

Some people have lots of friends online, but does that mean they are happy?

Having friends helps us to feel good. Friends laugh with us, and they share dreams and ideas. They listen to us when we feel upset, too. People with lots of friends on social networking sites always have someone to talk to online, so they don't feel bored. Moreover, when we have lots of friends, we feel important and special.

On the other hand, some people spend more time chatting to friends on the internet than they do in real life. Our online friends aren't always 'real' friends. Some people don't see their online friends very often.

In conclusion, having friends on social networking sites can help us to feel happy. However, we also need to have friends in real life. What's more, having one or two really good friends can be better than having lots of friends we don't know very well!

3 Read the essay again. Complete the table with the correct linking words.

Addition
¹ and   ² a.......................   ³ t.......................
⁴ M.......................
Contrast
⁵ b.......................   ⁶ H.......................
⁷ O.......................

Brain Trainer

Always make short notes before you write. Write down as many ideas as you can. Then choose the best ones.

Now do Exercise 4.

4a Read the essay title below. Are notes 1–6 for or against the topic?

Living in the countryside is important for happiness

1 living somewhere beautiful – feel happy *for*
2 more peaceful – less stressed   ....
3 less exciting – more boring   ....
4 meeting people and making friends – more difficult   ....
5 'green' places – good for health   ....
6 cinema, shops, etc. – travel a long way
....

b Do you agree?

5 You are going to write an essay with the same title. Complete the table with your ideas.

Paragraph 1: Introduction ....
....
Paragraph 2: Arguments for ....
....
Paragraph 3: Arguments against ....
....
Paragraph 4: Conclusion and your opinion ....
....

6 Now write your 'for and against' essay using the title in Exercise 4. Use the ideas and paragraph plan in Exercises 1–5. Include linking words of addition and contrast.

....
....
....
....
....
....
....
....

Check Your Progress 1

Grammar

1 Complete the email with the correct form of the verbs.

New Message   ⊗

Send

Hi there Kayla,

How's it going? I ^{0} *'ve been having* (have) an interesting day so far!

Earlier today, I ^{1} .... (go) into town to do some shopping. While I ^{2} ....
(walk) down Ash Street, I noticed a wallet on the ground. Luckily, there was a mobile number inside.

The owner, Chris, sounded delighted when I called. 'I ^{3} .... (look) for this wallet for hours and hours!' he said. We decided ^{4} .... (meet) in a café. When I first saw Chris he ^{5} .... (sit) with his back to me, so I didn't recognise him at first. But when I got closer I saw it was Chris Harper – you know, that awful boy we ^{6} .... (used to/hate) at primary school! He ^{7} .... (change) a lot since then. He ^{8} .... (not used to/ be) very friendly, but today I really enjoyed ^{9} .... (talk) to him. In fact, I ^{10} .... (think) about him non-stop since then. I hope he liked me too!

Anyway, call me soon. I think I need some advice about what to do next!

Eloise xx

/ 10 marks

2 Rewrite the second sentence so that it has a similar meaning to the first. Use between three and five words, including the word in brackets.

0 The last time I went surfing was two years ago. (been)
I *haven't been surfing for* two years.

1 I didn't like school when I was young. (use)
I .... school when I was young.

2 He moved to Lisbon two years ago. (living)
He .... for two years.

3 This is my first time on a steamboat! (never)
I .... on a steamboat before.

4 Having such amazing friends makes me feel lucky. (have)
I feel .... such amazing friends.

5 The last time I saw Sarah was Friday. (haven't)
I .... Friday.

/ 5 marks

Vocabulary

3 Choose the correct options.

I'm really sorry you're ^{0}*going* / *getting* / *giving* away. Please ^{1}*make* / *go* / *keep* in touch!

I'm bored and fed ^{2}*on* / *with* / *up*. Can I go and ^{3}*hang* / *keep* / *get* out with my friends?

Can you help? I'm looking ^{4}*at* / *for* / *to* my dog. He's ^{5}*gone* / *kept* / *made* missing!

/ 5 marks

4 Complete the definitions with suitable words.

0 A c*lassmate* is another student in your class.

1 When you feel embarrassed, you b........................ (your face goes red).

2 An a........................ is a place where planes land and take off.

3 Some people frown when they're in a bad m........................ .

4 If you k........................ calm, you don't panic or go crazy.

5 Each football team has one g........................ . He or she stands inside the goal.

/ 5 marks

5 Write the correct adjective or noun form of the word.

Historic figures

Leonardo da Vinci

Leonardo da Vinci was a very talented man! He was not only an [0] *artist* (art) but also a [1]........................ (sculpture), musician, scientist, mathematician, writer, [2]........................ (poem) – and quite a [3]........................ (wealth) businessman! Da Vinci's [4]........................ (beauty) painting of the Mona Lisa is probably the most [5]........................ (fame) portrait in the world.

/ 5 marks

Speaking

6 Complete the conversation with these words.

do	~~most~~	so (x2)	Sorry	story
such	to	true	way	would

Cal Hey, Leah, I've just heard the [0] *most* amazing piece of news!
Leah Really? What's the [1]........................ ?
Cal We've made it to the final of the school bands competition!
Leah No [2]........................ ! You're kidding me.
Cal Seriously, I swear it's [3]........................ . I was [4]........................ surprised when Tara told me, I think I gasped! She must think I'm [5]........................ an idiot.
Leah Probably …
Cal Thanks! So, anyway, [6]........................ you want to come round tonight to practise?
Leah [7]........................ . I'm going to have to say no. I've got [8]........................ much homework to do!
Cal Well, [9]........................ you like to come round on Saturday instead?
Leah I'd love [10]........................ . I'll see you then!

/ 10 marks

Translation

7 Translate the sentences.

1 We used to live in a farmhouse near a windmill.

....

2 Have you ever been on a speedboat or a motorbike?

....

3 The babysitter screamed while she was watching a horror film.

....

4 I want to find out how to help people and make a difference.

....

5 She's yawning because she's been looking after her little brother all day.

....

/ 5 marks

Dictation

8)) 11 Listen and write.

1 ....
2 ....
3 ....
4 ....
5 ....

/ 5 marks

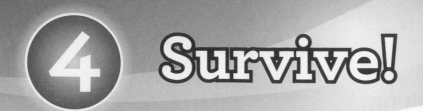

Survive!

Vocabulary Natural disasters

★ **1** Find natural disaster words in the word square. Then match the words to the definitions (1–8).

V	O	L	C	A	N	O	X	S	O	K
S	E	A	R	T	H	Q	U	A	K	E
R	B	O	G	U	H	T	J	R	A	H
I	A	V	A	L	A	N	C	H	E	G
Z	D	S	X	I	K	I	Q	G	H	J
C	H	P	N	D	I	S	E	A	S	E
Z	L	Z	C	Y	C	L	O	N	E	X
U	R	M	T	S	U	N	A	M	I	O
R	W	L	G	J	F	L	O	O	D	L
F	A	N	A	O	F	A	M	I	N	E

1 What happens when people die from hunger: f*amine*
2 A storm with very strong winds: c........................
3 A disaster that moves the earth: e........................
4 A very big, dangerous wave: t........................
5 A mountain that erupts: v........................
6 What happens when rivers and seas get too full: f........................
7 A bad illness that spreads from one person to another: d........................
8 What happens when snow or rocks fall down a mountain: a........................

Brain Trainer

When you learn new verbs, find out if they are regular or irregular. It is a good idea to record any irregular past forms, like this: *fall* (verb), *fell* (Past simple), *fallen* (Past participle).

Now do Exercise 2. Which verb has got an irregular past tense?

Vocabulary page 107

★ **2** Choose the correct options.

1 Some animals and plants can't *survive* / *spread* in very hot weather.
2 In 1928 Mount Etna *drowned* / *erupted* with smoke and hot, melted rocks.
3 Hot rocks and lava fell on Mascali and *buried* / *starved* the town in 1928.
4 In 1846–50, a million Irish people *starved* / *drowned* because they didn't have enough food.
5 When the Doña Paz hit another ship in 1987, 4,375 people *destroyed* / *drowned*.
6 The Great Fire of London *erupted* / *destroyed* 13,200 houses in 1666.

★★ **3** Match the captions (1–6) to the pictures (a–f). Then write the name of the natural disaster.

avalanche	drought	~~earthquake~~
famine	flood	volcano

1 It destroyed parts of the city.   .*f*.
   Disaster: ...*earthquake*....
2 Look! It's burying the village!   ....
   Disaster: ....
3 Help them They're starving!   ....
   Disaster: ....
4 It's erupting!   ....
   Disaster: ....
5 Save it before it drowns!   ....
   Disaster: ....
6 It didn't survive.   ....
   Disaster: ....

Reading

1 Read the article quickly. Choose the correct option to complete the first sentence.

   a … teaches people how to sail boats.

   b … saves lives at sea.

   c … researches extreme sea weather.

2 Read the article again and complete the fact file.

The RNLI: key facts

1 'RNLI' means *Royal National Lifeboat Institution*.

2 The RNLI helps people around Britain and ....

3 Around .... people volunteer for the charity.

4 RNLI has existed since ....

5 The charity owns around .... lifeboats.

6 It rescues around .... people every day.

---

3 Choose the correct options.

  1 What do we learn about the RNLI?

    a It's one of the four official emergency services in the UK.

    b It's one of the biggest British emergency services.

    c It doesn't pay any of the people who work for it.

  2 What do we learn about Joy?

    a She sometimes surprises people.

    b She joined the RNLI more than four years ago.

    c She is one of the first female volunteers.

  3 What do we learn about the UK?

    a It never has cyclones.

    b It sometimes has earthquakes.

    c It will never have a tsunami.

  4 What do we learn about tombstoning?

    a It is popular everywhere in the UK.

    b People try to jump onto rocks.

    c Some people have died after trying it.

4 Do you think Joy would agree with these statements? Write ✓ or ✗.

  1 I haven't got any heroes.   ✗

  2 I hope more women volunteer.

  3 I sometimes feel frightened.

  4 I think the RNLI costs far too much.

  5 I'm always happy at work.

  6 I always try to rescue everyone.

The fourth emergency service?

The Royal National Lifeboat Institution (RNLI) is a charity that …. . It operates around Britain and Ireland. After the police, fire and ambulance services, it's the largest emergency service in the UK, although not an official one. Many of the people who work for the RNLI volunteer for free.

Joy Thomas is one of around 40,000 volunteers. 'I've worked for the RNLI for almost four years,' she says. 'I've rescued over fifty people. At first, they're delighted to see me. But afterwards, they often express surprise. I think they expect to see an old man with a beard! However, 8% of RNLI lifeboat volunteers are women. As long ago as 1838, the amazing Grace Dent saved 13 people from drowning. More should follow her example!'

Since the RNLI began in 1824, it has saved more than 139,000 lives. That figure often shocks people, because the UK isn't famous for extreme weather. 'We don't often have cyclones, and we only experience tiny earthquakes, so tsunamis are unlikely,' says Joy, 'but that doesn't mean our coasts are safe, especially in storms and floods. Rescuers must be very careful, as sailing in these conditions is quite scary.'

The RNLI has to spend £385,000 every day on its 444 lifeboats and other services. 'But we save around 22 lives daily, which is worth any price', says Joy. 'And the people we rescue don't have to pay anything.'

'I'll help anyone in trouble,' she adds, 'but stupid behaviour does make me angry sometimes! In some parts of the country people go 'tombstoning' – they jump from high cliffs into the sea. They can't see the deep waters, or the rocks below. You really shouldn't try this dangerous hobby! Sadly, not everyone survives.'

Grammar Modals: ability, obligation, prohibition, advice

★ **1** Read the sentences (1–6). Match the verbs in bold to the meanings (a–f).

1 Luckily, I **can** climb quite well.   *b*
2 You **should** keep calm. You **shouldn't** panic.
3 I **can't** swim. Help!
4 We **must** leave now. We **have to** hurry!
5 You **don't have to** take the course if you don't want to.
6 You **mustn't** hunt the animals. It isn't allowed!

a obligation
b ability
c prohibition
d no ability
e advice
f no obligation

Brain Trainer

have to, *must*, *don't have to* and *mustn't* often cause problems for English learners. Write example sentences to help you to remember the differences.

must and *have to* = obligation
You **have to/must** wear a seatbelt. It's the law.
BUT *don't have to* = no obligation
You **don't have** (~~mustn't~~) **to** carry a first-aid kit. It's optional.
mustn't = prohibition
You **mustn't** (~~don't have to~~) drive without a licence. It's illegal.

Now do Exercise 2.

★ **2** Choose the correct options.

1 You .... go home. It's getting late.
   (a) should   b can   c mustn't
2 Help him! He .... swim!
   a shouldn't   b can't   c don't have to
3 You .... stay on the main path, but it's a good idea.
   a shouldn't   b mustn't   c don't have to
4 You .... go out without your mobile. What if you get lost?
   a don't have to   b can't   c shouldn't
5 We .... leave immediately. The tsunami is coming.
   a mustn't   b have to   c can
6 I've broken my leg. You .... leave me here on the mountain!
   a mustn't   b can   c don't have to

Past modals

★ **3** Complete the text with the Past simple of the verbs.

By the end of my first skiing holiday I ¹*could* (can) ski, but I ²........................ (can't) ski very fast! I ³........................ (have to) be careful, but I ⁴........................ (not have to) stay in the beginners area.

★★ **4** Complete the campsite notices. Choose the most suitable modal verb.

~~can~~	can	can't
could	don't have to	didn't have to
must	mustn't	should

① If you *can* ride a bike, why not join one of our cycling trips? (No excuses – if you .... ride a bike when you were five, you still .... now!)

② If you enjoy delicious food, you .... visit our café. We strongly recommend it!

③ You .... play music after 11 p.m. It's against camp rules.

④ You .... pay for maps. They're free!

⑤ Please don't use the pool if you .... swim.

⑥ You .... keep the campsite clea[n] and tidy, or we will ask you to pay a €20 fine. Last year our campers were all very responsib[le] and we .... fine anyone. Thank yo[u] for your cooperation! ☺

Grammar Reference pages 92–93

Vocabulary Phrasal verbs 2

1a Choose the correct prepositions.

1 I've run out *of* / *over* / *through* food. ☹
2 I got *down* / *on* / *through* all my exams with no problems.
3 I'm looking forward *to* / *off* / *on* tomorrow.
4 I've fallen *across* / *over* / *on*.
5 My motorbike has broken *down* / *over* / *out*.
6 I've worked *across* / *down* / *out* the answer.
7 I can't keep *on* / *through* / *over* going!
8 I was stressed at first, but now I've calmed *over* / *down* / *off*.

b Who is having problems? Write (☹).

2 Complete the calls for help with the correct form of these verbs.

break   come   fall   ~~get~~   run   work

1 **A** I'm so tired. I don't think I can *get* through this.
   B Yes, you can! Don't fall asleep. Help is coming.
2 **A** I'm lost! I can't .... out where I am.
   B Look around you. Tell me what you can see.
3 **A** We've just .... across a huge poisonous snake.
   B You mustn't go near it! Walk away slowly.
4 **A** My car has .... down on the motorway!
   B You should get out and wait in a safe place nearby.
5 **A** I've .... out of water.
   B Can you see a river or a pond anywhere?

3 Complete the text. Write one preposition in each gap.

We hope you're looking forward ¹*to* your camping holiday.

Don't forget to pack these essentials:

* a map and compass so you can always work ² .... where you are.
* a first-aid kit. It's useful if someone falls ³ .... or gets ill.
* lots of food so you don't run ⁴ .... Remember, the nearest shop might be kilometres away!
* suncream and a hat to put ⁵ .... if it's hot.
* a good camera or camera phone to take photos when you come ⁶ .... something interesting.

★★ 4 Answer the questions about the pictures. Use the correct form of a verb from list A and a preposition from list B to make phrasal verbs.

A	break	~~come~~	fall	put	run	take

B	~~across~~	down	off	on	out of	over

What's just happened?

1 I've just come across a snake.

2 She ....
....

3 Our ....
....

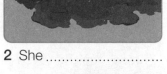

4 He ....
....

What's happening at the moment?

5 She ....
....

6 I ....
....

Vocabulary page 107

Chatroom Asking for clarification

Speaking and Listening

★ **1** What do we say *after* we've completely understood something?

   a Are you saying that … ?
   b Oh, I see!
   c What do you mean?

★ **2** 🔊 12 Complete the conversation with the correct form of these verbs. Then listen and check.

Hurry	mean	understand	say	see	~~swim~~

> **Jess** Hey, get out of the water! You shouldn't
>   ¹*swim* in the sea.
> **Rory** Sorry, I don't ² .... Are you
>   ³ .... that the sea is dangerous?
> **Jess** Yes! There are jellyfish!
> **Rory** What do you ⁴ .... ? Jellyfish
>   aren't dangerous.
> **Jess** Some kinds of jellyfish are! They can sting
>   you. It really hurts!
> **Rory** Oh, I ⁵ .... Thanks! OK, I'm
>   coming.
> **Jess** Good. ⁶ .... up!

★ **3** Match the phrases (a–f) to the gaps (1–6) in the conversation. What is the problem?

> **Ben** Stop!
> **Daisy** ¹*b* ! That hurt!
> **Ben** Sorry! ² ..... . I wanted to stop you before
>   you took a bite!
> **Daisy** Sorry, ³ ..... . What's the problem? ⁴ .... ?
>   I thought it was for everyone.
> **Ben** No, it isn't mine. But I should warn you –
>   Mum made it!
> **Daisy** ⁵ .... ? Does your mum want to eat it all?
> **Ben** No, but she's a terrible cook! You might
>   not survive.
> **Daisy** ⁶ .... . Thanks for the warning! I think I'll
>   have some crisps, then.

   a Are you saying that it's *your* cake
   b Ouch
   c Oh, I see
   d I don't understand
   e What do you mean
   f But you shouldn't eat that cake

★★ **4** 🔊 13 Listen to a conversation. Which image best matches Freya's map?

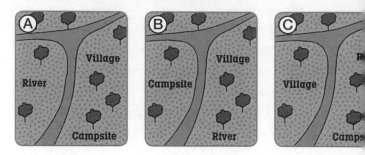

★★ **5** 🔊 13 Listen to the conversation again. Why does Jack say these statements? Match the statements (1–5) to the explanations (a–g). There are two explanations you don't need.

   1 Ouch!   *d*
   2 Hurry up!
   3 Are you saying that you want to go back
      to the campsite?
   4 It isn't right? What do you mean?
   5 Oh, I see. Thanks.

   a He doesn't understand why the sign is wrong.
   b He is feeling hungry.
   c He understands what Freya means.
   d He has hurt his foot.
   e He doesn't understand why Freya wants him
      to stop walking.
   f He disagrees that they need to phone for help.
   g He is feeling cold.

★★ **6** Write a conversation between two friends using the ideas below.

   • you / not drink from the river – dangerous
      ↓
      • sorry / not understand – you / say /
        dangerous animals / here?
        ↓
      • no / but water / not safe
        ↓
        • what / mean?
        ↓
   • dirty – sometimes people get diseases from /
      drink / dirty water
      ↓
        • oh / see! Thanks.

Speaking and Listening page 116

Grammar Modals: possibility

★ 1 Look at the photo. Then read the sentences (1–8). Does the writer think these things are possible (?), impossible (✗) or certain (✓)?

1 It might be a pet.   ?
2 He can't be frightened of spiders.
3 He could like other kinds of insects.
4 He must be quite brave!
5 It might run up his arm!
6 It must feel strange.
7 It can't be a poisonous spider.
8 It could bite him!

★ 2a Choose the correct options to complete the advert.

Storm Chaser Tours

Most holidays are quite similar. Perhaps you ¹(might)/ *must* go to the beach, or you ² *could / can't* visit a few museums. Yawn! Doing the same thing every year ³ *must / can't* be very exciting!

Chasing tornados ⁴ *can't / must* be one of the most exciting holiday experiences in the world. We're 100% sure! You'll see these amazing storms close up, and if you're lucky, you ⁵ *must / might* have some great photos to take home.

What's more, our tours are the cheapest in the USA. We ⁶ *can't / must* be crazy!

b Would you like this holiday? Why?/Why not?

Grammar Reference pages 92– 93

★★ 3 Complete the sentences about the photo with *might*, *must* or *can't*. Then answer the question below.

1 She *might* be in the Alps. I'm not sure.
2 She definitely .... be afraid of heights!
3 She .... enjoy climbing, or she wouldn't do it!
4 It looks very dangerous. There .... be an avalanche!
5 She .... be cold in all that snow!
6 Climbing that mountain .... be very easy. It looks impossible!
7 She .... feel frightened. We don't know.
8 Standing on the top of a mountain .... be an amazing feeling, that's for sure.

Which sentences can you rewrite with *could*?

★★ 4 Rewrite the sentences using *must*, *can't*, *might* or *could*. Sometimes there may be more than one correct answer.

1 It's possible it's a tsunami.
   It *could be a tsunami.*
2 I'm sure the disease is very painful.
   The disease ....
3 Perhaps the volcano is dangerous.
   The volcano ....
4 I'm not going to climb that mountain. Obviously, you think I'm an idiot!
   I'm not going to climb that mountain. You .... !
5 It's impossible for a drought to last forever.
   A drought ....
6 Maybe she's lost in the forest.
   She ....
7 I don't believe that anyone enjoys this awful weather – not even you!
   You .... ! I don't believe you!
8 I can't decide whether to get help.
   I .... I haven't decided yet.

Reading

1 Read the profile quickly. Find five animals.

1 f*ox*   4 w.......................
2 r.......................   5 f.......................h
3 a.......................   6 s.......................

PROFILE:

Ray Mears

survival expert

Ray Mears is an English TV star and survival expert. [a] .5. A young Ray wanted to explore local forests because he was very interested in animals, especially foxes. However, he couldn't afford camping equipment. [b] ....

In 1994, he appeared on his first TV programme. [c] .... These have been very popular because they're quite exciting. Ray doesn't just tell us how to survive. He shows us! On a typical show, we might see him digging for water in a drought, for example, or hunting a rabbit for supper.

Unlike other presenters, Ray is more interested in teaching us than shocking us. So he doesn't do crazy things, like wrestling alligators! He believes that people who want to survive mustn't do anything dangerous. However, we probably wouldn't want to try all of his ideas. Some of them aren't very pleasant! For instance, Ray believes that worms can be excellent food if you're hungry. [d] ....

Ray Mears believes that everyone should learn some basic survival skills. [e] .... For example, imagine you get lost on a walk. What would you do? On his UK survival courses, Ray teaches children and adults how to make a fire, find water and even catch fish amongst many other things!

In 2009, three young British tourists called Chiara, Rachel and Rory got lost in a forest in Malaysia. They were hungry, wet, and frightened of the dangerous snakes. Luckily, Rory liked watching TV! [f] .... The friends followed a river until it reached the coast, where they found help. They survived – thanks to Ray!

Brain Trainer

Writers often use pronouns and possessive adjectives (e.g. *I*, *she*, *ours*, *his*, *that*, *those*, *some*) to refer back to people, places, times and things which they have already mentioned. Read the previous sentences to find out what these pronouns and adjectives are referring to.

Now do Exercise 2.

2 Look at these missing sentences from the profile. What do the words in bold refer to? Use ideas from the box. Then match these sentences to the gaps (a–f) in the profile.

| ~~Ray Mears'~~ | 1994 | camping equipment |
| a worm | Rory | survival skills |

1 Instead, Ray worked out how to spend nights outside without **it** (.......................................)!
2 **He** (.......................................) remembered some advice from a Ray Mears' TV show.
3 But I don't think I'm going to try **one** (.......................................) very soon!
4 One day, **they** (.......................................) could save our lives!
5 **His** (*Ray Mears'*) interest in survival began in childhood.
6 Since **then** (.......................................), Ray's starred in over ten different shows.

Listening

1 🔊 14 Listen to four short recordings. Match the contexts (a–d) to the recordings (1–4).

a conversation between friends   *2*
b travel announcement
c instructions from a tour guide
d news programme

2 🔊 14 Listen again. Complete the problems with natural disaster words. Then complete the advice and warnings.

1 Problem: There's been a *flood*.
   Advice: People should travel *by bus*.
2 Problem: There's a ....
   Advice: People shouldn't ....
3 Problem: There's a ....
   Advice: People should ....
4 Problem: There's a .... in the area.
   Advice: People must ....

Writing Giving instructions

1 Read the travel advice quickly. Match the headings (a–e) to the gaps (1–3). There are two headings you don't need.

a After your trip   **d** What to pack
b Common problems   **e** During your trip
c How to prepare   *1*

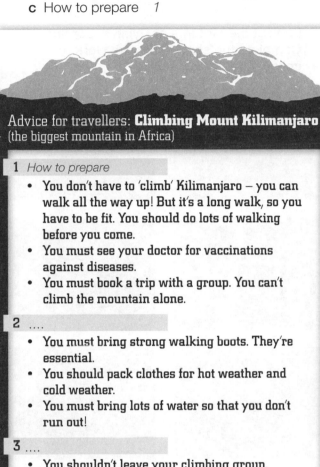

Advice for travellers: Climbing Mount Kilimanjaro
(the biggest mountain in Africa)

1 *How to prepare*
- You don't have to 'climb' Kilimanjaro – you can walk all the way up! But it's a long walk, so you have to be fit. You should do lots of walking before you come.
- You must see your doctor for vaccinations against diseases.
- You must book a trip with a group. You can't climb the mountain alone.

2 ....
- You must bring strong walking boots. They're essential.
- You should pack clothes for hot weather and cold weather.
- You must bring lots of water so that you don't run out!

3 ....
- You shouldn't leave your climbing group. It's dangerous!
- You should walk slowly and take rests. Climbing too quickly might make you feel very ill.
- Don't forget to have fun and take lots of photos of all the amazing things you come across!

2 How many bullet points (•) does the writer include in the information leaflet?

....

3 Think of an adventurous holiday that people do in your country. Choose one of the ideas below, or use your own idea.

walking/cycling in the mountains/desert/forest (Where?)

kayaking/sailing/surfing on a river/in the sea (Where?)

Your idea: ....

4 You are going to write an information leaflet like the one in Exercise 1. Complete the table with your ideas.

Advice for travellers: ....
(add your adventurous holiday idea)

Heading 1: How to prepare
Do travellers need any special skills? Do they need to do any training/research/ other preparation?   • ....   • ....   • ....
Heading 2: ....
What kind of clothes/other equipment do travellers need?   • ....   • ....   • ....
Heading 3: ....
Are there any dangers? What other problems might people have? Any other tips?   • ....   • ....   • ....

5 Now write your information leaflet using the title in Exercise 4. Use the ideas and paragraph plan in Exercises 1–4 and include a variety of modal verbs.

....
....
....
....
....
....
....
....
....
....
....
....
....
....
....
....
....
....
....

Work For It

Vocabulary Work collections

Brain Trainer

When you learn a new word, write down other words that collocate with it (*write emails, read emails, check emails*, etc.). It will help you to remember and use it correctly.

Now do Exercise 1.

★ **1** Write the missing parts of the work collocations. Then complete the crossword.

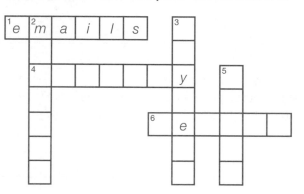

Across

1 I **checked** … at my computer.
4 I listened to her question and **dealt with** her … .
6 I **wrote** a … about the problem for my employer.

Down

2 I **attended** a long … in the afternoon.
3 I **took** a … of €100 from a customer.
5 I **answered the** … forty times today!

★ **2** Choose the correct options to complete the text.

I usually ¹(work)/ *attend* on reception at the hotel, but today I had to attend a big sales meeting. I went in early this morning and I ² *worked / prepared* lots of spreadsheets. I ran out of stationery so I ³ *prepared / ordered* some more. Then I ⁴ *did / gave* lots and lots of photocopying. After I ⁵ *dealt / gave* my presentation, I ⁶ *made / took* an appointment to see the doctor. I had a headache!

★★ **3** Look at the pictures of Dylan's morning. Complete the sentences with work collocations. Then answer the question.

1 At eight o'clock Dylan *attended a meeting*.
2 At nine o'clock he ....
3 At ten o'clock ....
4 At eleven o'clock ....
5 At twelve o'clock ....
6 At half past twelve ....

What happened at one o'clock? Why do you think it happened?

....

Vocabulary page 108

Reading

4 Stephanie is having a busy day! Complete her to-do list with the correct form of these verbs.

~~check~~	deal	Make
order	take	write

To-Do List

- Check emails to see who's coming to the party. URGENT!!!!
- .... an appointment to see the dentist.
- Buy a ticket for the concert! (Does the concert hall .... payments online?)
- .... English report for Monday. URGENT!!!
- Phone the supermarket about the job. Mrs Wilde .... with enquiries.
- Ask Mum to .... some more stationery online. This pen's running out

★ **1** Read the texts quickly. What kind of texts are they?

a letters b articles c adverts d reports

★ **2** Read the texts again. Complete the sentences. Write one word in each gap.

Job A
1 Work is available in the month of *August*.
2 You won't have to pay for eating ....
3 You will work for .... hours in total at the weekend.

Job B
4 There were .... bands in total last year.
5 You will work for .... hours in total at the weekend.
6 It's going to .... in August.

★★ **3** Which job would be best for someone who:

1 doesn't want to work every weekend? *B*
2 likes Spanish food?
3 speaks Spanish?
4 needs accommodation?
5 cares about the way they look?
6 has had a similar job before?

★★ **4a** Write the disadvantages of each job. Use *have to*, a suitable verb and the idea in brackets.

1 (early) *Waiters and waitresses have to get up early.*
2 (outside) ....
3 (for free) ....
4 (a uniform) ....

b Which job would you prefer?

A

Next Move Hotel

Work in our popular hotel café!

We need friendly, hard-working waiters and waitresses to work in our hotel café in August.

Language skills will be an advantage for dealing with orders, payments and enquiries, as we're going to have a large number of European visitors this summer. Our traditional British tea and cakes are internationally popular!

You'll work from 8.00 till 2.00 on Saturday, and 10.00 till 2.00 on Sunday. We'll provide two shirts with the hotel logo, which we'll expect you to keep clean. We'll reward hard workers with free breakfasts, in addition to their regular pay.

The café is going to be very busy, as the hotel is fully booked all August. For this reason, we're looking for waiters or waitresses who have had some previous experience.

Enquire at the reception desk for more details.

B

WANTED

FESTIVAL RUBBISH COLLECTORS

At this year's Teen Noise Festival we're going to have 65 amazing bands – 20 more than last year. We think it will be our best festival yet!

We're looking for English-speaking volunteers to work for six hours from midday on both Saturday 11th and Sunday 12th. No qualifications or experience are necessary. You'll collect rubbish from outside the international food quarter (selling everything from falafels to tapas!). The work is unpaid, but we'll give you free tickets and a place in a shared tent on the campsite.

You should bring boots, and clothes that you don't mind getting dirty, but we'll provide gloves. Bring a raincoat, too. We've seen the weather forecast for August, and it's going to be wet. Sorry!

To learn more, attend our Volunteer Information Meeting at the town hall at 19.00 on Monday 9th June.

TEEN NOISE FESTIVAL

Grammar *will/going to*

★ 1a Match John's comments and questions (1–6) to Lacey's replies (a–f). Then answer the question below.

John:
1 Have I got any meetings next Monday?   *e*
2 Have you finished that report yet?
3 Can you stay until 6.00 p.m. tomorrow, Lacey?
4 Is that your mobile phone?
5 What was the weather like when you went out for lunch?
6 We've run out of photocopy paper!

Lacey:
a I'm afraid not. I think I'll need another hour!
b Don't worry. I'll order some more.
c I'm sorry, I can't. I'm going to the hairdresser's.
d It was dark and windy. There's going to be a storm.
e Yes. You're going to meet Yola at 10.00 a.m.
f Sorry! I'll turn it off.

b How does John know Lacey?

a He works for her.
b He's her teacher.
c They're friends.
d She works for him.

★ 2 Choose the correct options to complete the conversations.

1 A Look out! You *re going to* / will drop that mug!
  B Oh no, too late! There's coffee all over the desk.
2 A It's cold in this office.
  B I*'m going to* / *'ll* close the door.
3 A Do you fancy doing something after work?
  B I can't. I*'m going to* / *'ll* study tonight.
4 A I'm worried about the presentation.
  B I'm sure you*'re going to* / *'ll* do really well.
5 A Oh no! We've missed the train.
  B We*'re going to* / *'ll* be late for work!
6 A Who do you think *is going to* / *will* get the job?
  B I really don't know.

★★ 3 Complete the conversation with the correct form of the verbs.

A ¹ *Are you going to finish* (you/finish) work soon, Jake? You've been working hard all day!
B I know, but I ² .... (give) a big presentation tomorrow. I need to prepare some spreadsheets, but they're really difficult! I ³ .... (try) to stop soon, I promise.
A I ⁴ .... (help) you, if you like.
B Really? It probably ⁵ .... (not be) much fun!
A I don't mind. Look at that sky. It ⁶ .... (be) dark soon. You can't work all night!

★★ 4 Are the verbs in bold correct (✓) or incorrect (✗)? Correct the mistakes.

1 It's really cold! It **will snow**.   ✗
  's going to snow
2 I**'m going to get** a job this summer.
  ....
3 Look out! We**'ll crash**!
  ....
4 In ten years' time I think I**'ll be** famous.
  ....
5 A These books are heavy!
  B I**'m going to help** you.
  ....
6 She **will see** the band tonight. She's already bought a ticket.
  ....

★★ 5 Complete these sentences. Use the correct form of *will* or *going to* and a suitable verb.

1 I think I*'ll win* the lottery one day. I feel lucky!
2 Look at those dark clouds! It ....
3 A It's hot in here!
  B I .... a window.
4 In two years' time, Ash .... science at university.
5 You've missed the bus! You .... late for school.
6 Marta .... an important meeting this afternoon.
7 In 2100, I think robots .... most of our work for us.
8 A The phone's ringing! I .... it.
  B Thanks!

Grammar Reference pages 94–95

Vocabulary Job qualities

★ **1** Complete the job qualities. Write the vowels (*a, e, i, o, u*).

    1 Car mechanics must be pr_a_ct_i_c_a_l.
    2 Nurses must be very r_l_ _bl_ .
    3 Scientists should be _n_lyt_c_l.
    4 Footballers must be good t_ _m pl_y_rs.
    5 Teachers should be g_ _d c_mm_n_c_t_rs.
    6 Politicians must have good l_ _d_rsh_p qu_l_t_ _s.

★ **2** Put the letters in the correct order to make adjectives.

> **Reference: Morgan Godwin**
>
> Morgan is an ¹ *experienced* (nexreipcde) computer programmer who has worked for us for two years. He has ² e .... (xetcenll) IT skills. He is very ³ p .... (attine) when it comes to working out the answers to long, difficult problems, and his work is almost always ⁴ a .... ractcue), with few mistakes. He is very p .... tuaulnc), and he is never late for work. His work is always very efficient and o .... (esinagrd), and you can rely on him to plan his time well. We will be very sad to say 'goodbye'!

★ **3** Complete the table. Write the positive job qualities.

| accurate | a good communicator | analytical |
| a team player | ~~patient~~ | punctual |

Work 'dos' and 'don'ts'!	
DON'T	**DO**
try to do everything quickly.	be ¹ *patient*.
be late!	be ² ....
make lots of mistakes.	be ³ ....
keep all your ideas to yourself.	be ⁴ ....
be competitive and refuse to help others.	be ⁵ ....
accept information without thinking about it.	be ⁶ ....

Vocabulary page 108

★★ **4a** Complete the article.

communicator	experienced	leadership
organised	patient	punctual
~~reliable~~	skills	

So you think it's easy to be a celebrity?

Think again! If you want to be famous, you should:

★ be ¹ *reliable*. People won't give you work if they can't trust you.

★ get as much useful experience as you can! ² .... people are much more likely to succeed.

★ be ³ .... You need a good diary to plan your time!

★ be a good ⁴ .... , so you can do well in interviews.

★ have good IT ⁵ .... Social networking and blogging will keep you in touch with your fans.

★ be ⁶ .... It's OK for Rihanna to be late, but not for 'smaller' stars!

★ have ⁷ .... qualities, so that people want to work for you.

★ be ⁸ .... Becoming famous takes time!

b What other qualities do you think celebrities need?

....

 **Phone language**

Speaking and Listening

★ 1 Put the conversation in the correct order.

a Yes please. My name is Aimee Fisher, and … ....

b Oh hello. I'm calling about the advertisement for a pool lifeguard. Can I speak to the manager? ....

c How do you spell that? Oh, hold on. Omar's just come in. I'll pass you over to him. Just a moment. ....

d Hello. Garforth Leisure Centre here. How can I help you? *.1..*

e You need to speak to Omar, but he isn't here at the moment. Can I take a message? ....

★ 2 🔊 15 **Choose the correct options. Then listen and check.**

A Hello, Ballymore Books here.

B Good afternoon. I ¹*like /*(*'d like*)to speak to the manager, please.

A Who's calling?

B My name is Harry Blaine. I'm calling ²*about / for* the job interview I attended last week.

A ³*Keep / Hold* on please. I'll ⁴*put / give* you through to her now.

B Thank you!

A Just a ⁵*moment / while*. Oh dear … I'm afraid she's in a meeting. Would you like to call back later, or can I ⁶*make / take* a message?

★ 3 🔊 16 **Listen to a phone conversation. Then answer the questions.**

1 How many managers are there at Electric Records? *two*

2 What job is Ivy interested in? ....

3 On which day of the week would Ivy need to work? ....

4 Where is Faith? ....

5 What is Ivy's full name? ....

6 What is her phone number? ....

★★ 4 🔊 16 **Complete the expressions in the table. Listen again and cross (✗) the expression you don't hear.**

Saying why you're calling
I'd ¹*like* to speak to … ☐
I'm ²c........................ about … ☐
Asking someone to wait
³J........................ a moment. ☐
⁴H........................ on, please. ☐
Transferring a call
I'll ⁵p........................ you through (to him/her) now. ☐
I'll pass you ⁶........................ to him/her. ☐
Offering to give someone a message
Can I ⁷t........................ a message? ☐

★★ 5 Write a phone conversation like the ones in Exercises 1–3. Use these ideas and the phone language in Exercise 4.

- You are calling about a job. (What job?) You want to speak to the manager.
- The manager is not there. (Where is he/she?)
- You leave a message. (What's your name and phone number?)
- The manager returns. The person you are speaking to transfers your call.

Speaking and Listening page 117

Grammar Present simple and Present continuous for future

★ **1** Read the sentences. Write *DP* for definite plans and *SE* for scheduled events.

1 The office closes at 6.00.   *SE*
2 My mum isn't working tomorrow.   ....
3 The concert starts at 7.45.   ....
4 The shops open at 8.30.   ....
5 Are you studying tonight?   ....
6 I'm going home soon.   ....

★ **2** Choose the correct options.

Tomorrow morning I ¹*work* / *'m working* at the café. I ²*get* / *'m getting* up early, because the café ³*opens* / *is opening* at 8.30, and my bus ⁴*leaves* / *is leaving* at 7.46! I'm not going to work all day. After lunch, I ⁵*meet* / *'m meeting* my friend Kate in town. We ⁶*see* / *'re seeing* a film. It ⁷*starts* / *'s starting* at 2.00 and it ⁸*ends* / *'s ending* at 4.50. It's a very long film, so I hope it's good!

★ **3** Complete the text. Use the correct Present simple or Present continuous form of these verbs.

deal	finish	have got	not go	open
relax	start	~~work~~	you/do	

This Saturday is going to be a busy day. I ¹*'m working* at the museum all day. Work ²........................ at 8.30, and the museum ³........................ to visitors at 9.00. On Saturday I ⁴........................ with enquiries at the information desk. I ⁵........................ a short lunch break at 12.30, but it ⁶........................ at 1.00! In the evening I ⁷........................ out. I ⁸........................ at home with my family. What ⁹........................ this Saturday?

Grammar Reference pages 94–95

★★ **4** Read the notes in Aiden's diary. Write sentences using the ideas and the correct form of the Present simple or Present continuous.

Thursday

Friday

Friday evening –
video games with Briony

Saturday

the BEACH, all day!!!
8.55 bus
Saturday evening – at cousins' house

Sunday

train – 09.11, home 09.45
football practice 2.00
Sunday evening – nothing!

1 Friday evening / he / play
On Friday evening he's playing video games with Briony.
2 Saturday / he / spend / all day
....
....
3 Saturday / the bus / leave
....
....
4 Saturday evening / he / stay
....
....
5 Sunday / train / arrive / home
....
....
6 Sunday afternoon / he / play
....
....
7 Sunday / football practice / start
....
....
8 Sunday evening / he / not do
....
....

Reading

1 Read the article quickly. Choose the best heading.

   a The best jobs in the world?
   b Jobs for students
   c Three jobs I've tried

2 Complete the article. Match the personal qualities (a–f) to the gaps (1–6).

   a friendly   **d** patient
   b a good communicator   **e** adventurous
   c punctual   **f** analytical

3 Are the sentences true (T), false (F) or don't know (DK)?

   1 This article is for people who've left school. *F*
   2 The best video games testers become video game designers. ....
   3 Testers will have to play lots of different games every week. ....
   4 There are thousands of successful music critics. ....
   5 Music critics often get music for free. ....
   6 Ice cream tasters get up before 6 a.m. every day. ....
   7 You can try tea-flavoured ice cream in Japan. ....

Ideal jobs

| HOME | NEWS | FEATURES | PHOTOS | COMMENTS |

Have you decided what you're going to do after you leave school or university? Read about our three favourite dream jobs, and you might change your mind!

A VIDEO GAME TESTER

What are you doing this weekend? If your answer includes the words 'playing video games', then this might be the right job for you. But being good at gaming isn't the only skill you'll need! Being ¹ *f.* is essential, as game designers want you to notice all possible problems to help them to work out solutions. Being ² .... is almost as important. You'll spend weeks and even months playing the same game.

B MUSIC CRITIC

Are you going to attend any concerts or festivals this summer? Imagine that you could make money at the same time by writing reviews! Thousands of people want this job, but only a tiny number will be successful. You'll need to work hard and be very talented. It's important to be ³ ...., so that musicians will like you. And you must be ⁴ .... . If you're late, bands won't wait for you! It's worth the effort, though. You'll have some amazing experiences, and you'll probably hardly ever pay for music again!

C ICE CREAM TASTER

Yes, this is a real job! We asked official 'taster' Rob Browning what skills you need. 'Well, you have to be ⁵ ...., because you'll need to write long reports. And I hope you're an ⁶ .... person who loves travel and doesn't mind a few early mornings! Tomorrow, I'm flying to Tokyo – my plane leaves at 5.23! I've tasted popular flavours all over the world. Tomorrow, that means green tea ice cream! I've also tried Mexican chilli, and – less enjoyably – cheese flavour in the Philippines!'

Listening

1 🔊 17 Listen to two job interviews. Cameron and Erin want the same job. What is it?

   .... instructor

2 🔊 17 Listen again. Who has these qualities, skills and experience? Write *C* (Cameron), *E* (Erin) or *B* (both of them).

   Who ...
   1 is really interested in sport? *B*
   2 has studied the subject? ....
   3 has done similar work before? ....
   4 has worked with people of all ages? ....
   5 is a patient person? ....
   6 enjoys hard work? ....

3 Who do you think is best for the job? Why?

   ....
   ....
   ....
   ....
   ....

Writing An email about plans

1 Read Ben's email quickly. What are the *two* main things he's going to do this summer? Complete the sentences.

   1 He's going to work in a ....

   2 He's going to go to ....

New Message ⊗

Send

Hi there,

How are you? How's school? Things are going well here, but I'm definitely looking forward to the holidays!

I've got lots of plans for the summer. For a start, I've got a job! My aunt says I can help her in the bookshop, which will be great, because I love books. It will certainly be much more interesting than the office job I did last year. I think I probably spent most of my time doing photocopying.

What else? Oh yes – we're also going to have a family holiday in Rome. That will definitely be amazing. I don't know what we're going to do yet. Maybe we'll explore the area, or perhaps we'll do lots of shopping. We're certainly going to visit the art galleries. You know Dad's crazy about art! I'll probably send you a postcard. ☺

What are you doing this summer? Write and tell me about your plans!

Ben x

PS Some photos of Rome attached! Can't wait!

Add Attachments: ⊗   **Add Attachments:** ⊗

---

2 Read the letter again and find five adverbs of certainty. Complete the table.

100% sure	¹ c *ertainly* ² d........................
less sure	³ p........................
don't know	⁴ m........................ ⁵ p........................

3 Write sentences. Use short forms (*we're, isn't,* etc.) where possible and include the adverbs.

   1 we / will / see / you / there / !   (maybe)
   Maybe we'll see you there!

   2 we / will / go / to the beach   (I think)
   ....

   3 My brother / work / too hard   (definitely)
   ....

   4 It / be / very / hot   (certainly)
   ....

   5 I / be / going to / do / some studying   (probably)
   ....

   6 you / will / visit / us / !   (perhaps)
   ....

⚙ **Brain Trainer**

When you write to friends or people you know well, use an informal, conversational style. Use informal expressions (*Hi there! … crazy about art*, etc.) and short forms (*I'm, he'll, won't*, etc.)

Now do Exercise 4.

---

4 Write a letter to a friend about your plans for the summer. You can use your real plans or you can make them up. Use some of the ideas in the list or your own ideas. Include at least three different future forms in your letter.

a summer job	a holiday
plans with friends	plans for relaxation
school work	family events (*birthdays*, etc.)
hobbies (*sport events*, *music events*, *courses*, etc.)	

....
....
....
....
....
....
....
....
....
....
....
....
....
....
....

6 Coast

Vocabulary Coastal life

★ **1** Tick (✓) five things connected with the coast.

1 caretaker
2 fish and chip shop ✓
3 spaceship
4 avalanche
5 pier
6 cliff
7 spreadsheet
8 harbour
9 ice cream kiosk

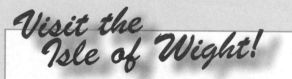

Brain Trainer

We can form compound nouns in different ways: as one word (*classroom*), as separate words (*reception desk*) or as separate words connected with a hyphen (*T-shirt*). Use a dictionary to check the correct spelling.

Now do Exercise 2.

★ **2** Match (1–7) to (a–g). Then write the compound nouns.

1 sea
2 sea
3 deck
4 beach
5 amusement
6 souvenir
7 go

a hut
b gull
c kart
d shop
e arcade
f wall
g chair

1 *sea wall*
2 ....
3 ....
4 ....
5 ....
6 ....
7 ....

★★ **3** Complete the advertisements. Which place would you rather visit?

amusement arcades	beach huts
cliffs	deckchairs
fish and chip shops	harbours
~~piers~~	souvenir shops

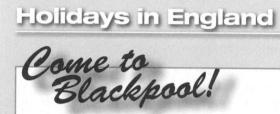

Holidays in England

Come to Blackpool!

The three famous, long ¹*piers* at Blackpool were built for fun and excitement!
As well as theme park rides, they offer ² .... where you can play games, ³ .... where you can buy presents, and excellent ⁴ .... where you can enjoy fresh food from the sea.

Visit the Isle of Wight!

Walk along the top of the beautiful, wild ⁵ .... and look down for amazing views of the sea. Admire the boats sailing into the famous ⁶ .... at Cowes and Yarmouth.

Or families may prefer simply to sit on ⁷ .... on the beach and relax! Visitors have a choice of accommodation in hotels, campsites or ⁸ ....

Vocabulary page 109

Reading

★ **1** Read the reviews quickly. Are the reviewers:

a professional travel writers?
b tourists who've been on holiday?

★ **2** Read the reviews again. Who talks about these things? Write A–D.

1 the accommodation: A , ... , ...
2 the people who work there: .... , ...
3 the washing facilities: .... , ...
4 the food: .... , ...
5 the cost: .... , ... , ...
6 the views: .... , ...

Brain Trainer

Sometimes questions use different words from the text. Think about synonyms (words with similar meanings).

Now do Exercise 3.

★ **3a** Match the words in bold in the sentences to these synonyms.

| budget | close | loud | ~~modern~~ |
| ordinary | pleasant | tasty | welcoming |

1 Joanne stayed in **new** (= *modern*) accommodation.   T
2 Joanne thinks that the food was better than **average** (= ....).   ....
3 Danny thinks that the people at the resort were very **friendly** (= ....).   ....
4 Danny thinks that the resort serves the most **delicious** (= ....) food in Whitby.   ....
5 Keith says that the sea wasn't very **near** (= ....).   ....
6 Keith did not find any part of his holiday **enjoyable** (= ....).   ....
7 Atena thinks that the resort was sometimes too **noisy** (= ....).   ....
8 Atena thinks that it's a **cheap** (= ....) holiday.   ....

b Use the word clues in Exercise 3a to find the matching parts of the text. Are the sentences true (T) or false (F)?

★ **4** Match the ratings (1–4) to the reviews (A–D).

1 ●○○○   ....   3 ●●●○   ....
2 ●●○○   ....   4 ●●●●   ....

Bayley's Holiday Resort
(north of Whitby)

Reviews from holidaymakers | Write a review

4 reviews sorted by date

Ⓐ **Joanne R, Australia**   Reviewed 17 July

The showers were broken on the first night that I arrived, but they were repaired the next day. I wanted to stay in one of the lovely old beach huts, but they were full, so in the end I stayed in a modern caravan. It wasn't too bad, though. I'd describe the meals as fairly ordinary, but the service from waiters and resort assistants is above average. However, the resort prices are too high.

Ⓑ **Danny O, England**   Reviewed 29 July

We stayed for seven days. The only regret I have is that I couldn't take a longer break from work! It would be impossible to find more welcoming staff anywhere. The showers and toilets were cleaned regularly. The restaurant fish suppers are almost as tasty as those which are served in the famous Whitby fish and chip shops – and that's a big recommendation!

Ⓒ **Keith McD, Scotland**   Reviewed 04 August

I was promised a camping place where I could see the cliffs, but instead my tent faced the road. On the website, the beach is described as 'close'. This isn't true. I did a lot of walking! There are no snack bars or ice cream kiosks at the resort. I spent most of my time in Whitby, which had some lovely cafés and souvenir shops. That's my only pleasant memory!

Ⓓ **Atena J, Greece**   Reviewed 23 August

We stayed in the pretty campsite area. Unfortunately we didn't sleep well, though, because the seagulls were very loud! Next time I'll book one of the beach huts, where guests can see the sea from their windows. Apparently, more huts will be built next year, which is good news. It isn't a budget resort, but you do get good value for money. Apart from the gulls, I'd describe it as *almost* perfect!

Grammar Passive statements

★ **1** Choose the correct options (active or passive) to complete the sentences.

1 Most of the world's biggest cities ~~established~~ / (were established) within 100 km of the sea.

2 The coastline of Canada *measures / is measured* more than 200,000 km in length.

3 By 2500, thousands more homes *will build / will be built* near the coast.

4 Rising sea levels *will make / will have made* floods a big problem in the future.

5 Many coasts *pollute / are polluted* with rubbish.

6 Last year around one million sea birds *killed / were killed* by plastic rubbish.

★ **2a** Complete the sentences with the correct passive form of the verbs.

True or false?

1 Caviar *is made* (make) from fish eggs.

2 The first steamboat .... (invented) in the 1700s.

3 The island of Atlantis .... (will visit) by 1,000,000 tourists next year.

4 Over 70% of the Earth .... (cover) in water.

5 The Titanic .... (discovered) at the bottom of the ocean in 1960.

6 Thousands of people .... (will kill) by sea scorpions next year.

b Which sentences do you think are true? Check your answers below.

Brain Trainer

Use *by* + agent if it is important to say who or what does the action. (The city was built *by the Romans*.) Don't use *by* if the agent is unimportant. (The wall was painted red ~~by someone~~.)
Now do Exercise 3.

★★ **3** Rewrite the sentences in the passive. Include *by* + agent only when it is necessary.

1 People will build thousands more homes in Bournemouth in the future.
Thousands more homes *will be built in Bournemouth in the future.*

2 In 2012, people named Bournemouth the UK's best beach destination.
In 2012, Bournemouth ....

3 People describe the town as one of the happiest places in the UK!
The town ....

4 J.R.R. Tolkien and Robert Louis Stevenson admired Bournemouth.
Bournemouth ....

5 Bournemouth's pretty beaches attract many visitors.
Many visitors ....

6 This summer, over 100,000 people will visit Bournemouth.
This summer, Bournemouth ....

7 In March 2012, Stuart Murdoch built an 8.5 metre high beach deckchair!
In March 2012, an 8.5 metre high deckchair ....
....

★★ **4** Complete the texts about three coastal festivals with the correct Present simple, Past simple or *will* future form of the verbs in the active or passive.

Ⓐ The amazing Benicàssim Music Festival [1] *is held* (hold) close to the beaches of Valencia, Spain, every year. It [2] .... (know) for being one of the best pop music festivals in Europe! Over 50,000 people [3] .... (attend) every year. The next festival [4] .... (organise) in July.

Ⓑ Part of the coast in Queensland, Australia, [5] .... (name) 'Surfers' Paradise' in 1933! Next year's surfing festival [6] .... (have) parades, parties, and surfing competitions. Many hotels [7] .... (book) months in advance – so don't wait!

Ⓒ The first oyster festival [8] .... (celebrate) in Arcata Bay, USA, over 22 years ago. Visitors [9] .... (eat) thousands of oysters last year! Today, all the oysters [10] .... (catch) using environmentally-friendly fishing methods.

Grammar Reference pages 96–97

Vocabulary Verbs with prefixes *dis-* and *re-*

★ **1** Form verbs by adding the prefix *dis-* or *re-*. One word stem can make two new forms.

1 *dis*appear
2 *re*place
3 ....continue
4 ....like
5 ....lease
6 ....cover OR ....cover
7 ....move
8 ....agree
9 ....search
10 ....store

★ **2** Choose the correct options for the definitions.

1 study in detail: *discover / research / restore*
2 have a different opinion: *dislike / disagree / recover*
3 take something away: *remove / recover / disappear*
4 stop making something: *restore / release / discontinue*
5 find: *restore / discover / recover*

★ **3** Choose the correct options.

1 Help! I've deleted all my files on my laptop and I can't .... them!
  a discontinue **b** recover **c** remove

2 I .... crowded beaches. I prefer peaceful places!
  a disagree **b** remove **c** dislike

3 We .... the history of the coast online.
  a researched **b** recovered **c** restored

4 I was upset when they .... my favourite ice cream flavour.
  a restored
  b disappeared
  c discontinued

5 I can't .... the ugly stain on this deckchair!
  a remove **b** discontinue **c** disturb

6 The builders .... the sea wall after it was damaged.
  a disappeared **b** restored **c** released

7 We .... an unusual museum near the harbour.
  a released **b** recovered **c** discovered

8 We .... the seagull back into the wild.
  a recovered **b** replaced **c** released

★★ **4** Complete the text with the correct form of the verbs. Would you support this charity?

| disagree | disappear | discontinue | discover |
| recover | release | research | restore |

SAVE OUR WHALES!

Whales are the biggest and best-loved creatures on the planet, but they're [1] *disappearing* from our seas. Soon, there may be so few that whale populations will never [2] ....

● Sadly, our research teams have [3] .... that some people are still hunting whales. We completely [4] .... with whale hunting. It's wrong! We think it should [5] .... immediately, ending forever.

● Instead, we need to [6] .... whale habitats and food, to work out how to help them.

● Many seas and oceans are polluted – we must [7] .... them to clean environments for whales to live in.

● Finally, we should [8] .... all whales in aquariums and sea parks back into the wild.

Please support our charity if you agree.

★★ **5** Complete the sentences. Use verbs which begin with the prefixes *dis-* or *re-*. Which sentences are true for you?

1 I hate it when people touch, disturb or re*move* my things without permission!
2 I love beach holidays but I dis........................ city holidays.
3 I usually re........................ my school projects online to find out more information.
4 Some people think shopping is boring, but I dis........................ with them.
5 I think the best way to re........................ quickly from a cold is to drink lots of water.
6 I think we should re........................ zoo animals back into the wild.
7 I like to dis........................ new places on holiday and do new things.
8 I don't like my mobile. I want to re........................ it with a new one.

Vocabulary page 109

Chatroom Asking for and giving directions

Speaking and Listening

★ **1** Choose the correct options.

A Excuse me. Could you ¹*say / tell* me where the beach is?

B ²*Cross / Go* over the road by the art gallery.
³*Take / Turn* the first right. You can't
⁴*lose / miss* it!

A Excuse me, could you ⁵*direct / get* me to the aquarium?

B Certainly. ⁶*Take / Turn* left out of here. Go
⁷*over / past* the souvenir shops. Then take the
third ⁸*taking / turning* on the right. It's on the left!

★ **2** 〔 18 〕 Listen and read. Is the information in bold correct (✓) or incorrect (✗)? Correct the mistakes.

A Excuse me. How do I get to
¹**Thomas Road** ✗ *Thomas Avenue*?

B Turn ²**left out of here** ....
and then take ³**the third left**
.... Cross over the
road. Then take ⁴**the first turning on the left**
.... Go
⁵**past St Mary's Street**
.... Then take
⁶**the next right** ....
Thomas Avenue is ⁷**opposite the post office**
.... You can't miss it!

★★ **3** 〔 19 〕 Look at the map. Listen to the conversation and try to follow the directions on the map. Answer the questions.

1 Where are the girl and the man now?
....

2 Where does the girl want to go?
....

3 How long will it take her to get there?
....

4 Which *three* streets or roads does she need to walk down? (Write the names from the map)
.... , ... and
....

★★ **4** 〔 19 〕 Listen again. Complete the question and the directions. Write one word in each gap.

1 Excuse me. *Could* you d...................... me to
the ...., please?

2 T...................... l...................... out of here.

3 C...................... o...................... the road
by the ....

4 T...................... the second ....
on the ....

5 Go p...................... the ....

6 It's o...................... the left. You can't
m...................... it!

★★ **5** Look at the map again. Decide where you are now and where you want to go. Then write a conversation asking for and giving directions.

Speaking and Listening page 118

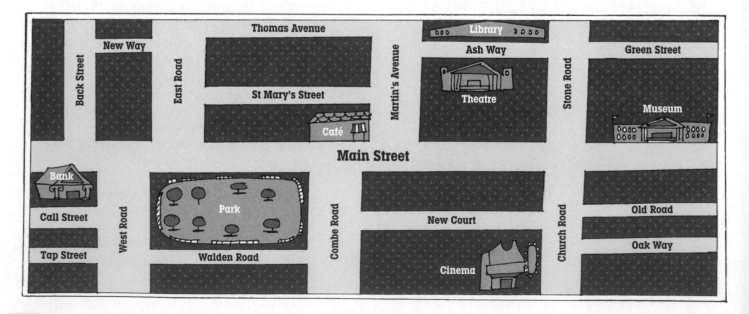

★ 54 ▶

Grammar Passive questions

★ 1 Complete the passive questions. Then answer the question below.

1 Traditionally, which pets *are kept* by pirates?
Traditionally, parrots are kept by pirates.

2 What .... the pirate in Peter Pan .... ?
He is called Captain Hook.

3 How much sunken treasure .... in the future?
We don't know how much sunken treasure will be discovered in the future.

4 Who .... Captain Jack Sparrow .... by?
He was played by Johnny Depp.

5 In fiction, where .... bad pirate captains often .... ?
They are often left alone on an island!

6 In the past, what kind of food .... usually .... by pirates at sea?
Biscuits and dried meat were usually eaten by .... pirates at sea.

What are all these questions about?
They're ....

★ 2 Put the words in the correct order to make passive questions.

1 When the / island / discovered / was / ?
When was the island discovered?

2 made / ice cream / the / here / Is / ?
.... ?

3 the / sold / When / beach huts / were / ?
.... ?

4 the / be / shark / caught / Will / ?
.... ?

5 cooked / How / fish / the / is / ?
.... ?

6 will / be / Where / arcade / built / the / ?
.... ?

★★ 3a Complete the questions using the Present simple, Past simple or *will* future passive forms.

SEA LIFE QUIZ

1 What animals *are penguins hunted* by in the wild? (penguins/hunt)
   a sharks   b blue whales   c crocodiles

2 What .... from? (pearls/make)
   a fish   b sand   c plants

3 Who .... by in 1975? (the first *Jaws* film/direct)
   a James Cameron   b George Lucas
   c Steven Spielberg

4 It's a famous book about a whale. But who .... by in 1851?
(*Moby Dick*/write)
   a Henry James   b Herman Melville
   c Charles Dickens

5 What .... by next year? (20% of sea turtles/kill)
   a boats   b whales   c plastic bags

6 Where .... tomorrow? (most shark soup/eat)
   a China   b the USA   c Africa

b Read the quiz again. Can you guess the correct answers? Check your answers below.

★★ 4 Write passive questions for the information in bold.

1 *When will the sea wall be repaired*?
They will repair the sea wall **next week**.

2 .... ?
They will release the seagull **on the cliff**.

3 .... ?
People catch the whales **by boat**.

4 .... ?
People visited the harbour **because it was famous**.

Grammar Reference pages 96– 97

Reading

1 Read the email quickly. Put the places Casey visited in the correct order.

   a a tall building   ....

   b a theme park   _1_

   c a beach restaurant   ....

   d a wild reef   ....

New Message   ⊗

Hi Morgan,   **Send**

How are things? I'm having an amazing time in Queensland, Australia!

On Monday we went to Sea World. Going on the rides was quite good fun, but the real attraction was seeing the animals. Wow! As well as dolphins and sharks, there were three polar bears, and stingrays, too, which you can feed. I wouldn't recommend touching the stingrays, though. *I did* – it wasn't pleasant! There's also a seabird hospital, where injured birds are looked after. When they're well, they'll be released.

On the next day we climbed Q1, which is a very tall skyscraper by the coast. Builders started work in 2002, and they finished three years later! The views were pretty cool. But the climb was terrifying. We had to go up the *outside* of the building. Never again!

On Wednesday, I saw the Great Barrier Reef. The sailboat ride there was OK, but a bit slow. However, the reef was so beautiful I didn't mind. Our guide said you can see it from space! It was quite sad, though, because parts of the reef are dying. Pollution will probably destroy the reef within fifty years, and we won't be able to restore it.

I went surfing all day yesterday! I read that about one in every ten Australians surf, and it's probably my favourite sport, too. Mum went to the souvenir shops instead, but Dad had his first lesson. It was really funny – for me! He fell over *a lot*.

Afterwards, we ate something called 'surf and turf' at this great place near the beach. That's seafood with steak. It's not bad, but you need to be hungry! We ordered it because we thought it was a typical Australian dish. But it's actually from the USA!

I hope you're having a good summer! See you soon,

Casey x

---

2 Read the email again. Which of these activities did Casey really like (☺☺), quite like (☺) or dislike? (☹).

   1 going on rides   ☺

   2 seeing sea animals

   3 holding a sea animal

   4 climbing

   5 sailing

   6 doing an adventurous sea sport

   7 trying new food

3 Complete the sentences with information from the text. Use the correct passive form of the verbs where given.

   1 *Three* polar bears *are kept* (keep) at Sea World.

   2 Q1........................ (build) in the years 2002 to ....

   3 It's possible that the Great Barrier Reef .... (destroy) in the next .... years.

   4 Surf and Turf is an .... dish which .... (make) with meat and ....

   5 The sport of .... (enjoy) by about .... % of Australians.

Listening

1 🔊 **20**   Listen to a speaker talking about the Giant's Causeway. What is the recording?

   a an advertisement

   b a conversation

   c a presentation

2 🔊 **20**   Listen again. Match the dates and numbers (1–8) to the things they refer to (a–h).

   1 350,000   *e*   **5** 200

   2 40,000   **6** 1,300

   3 1967   **7** 1.25

   4 1.8   **8** 1986

   a year it became a World Heritage site

   b distance from Belfast in hours

   c number of rocks

   d number of kinds of plants and birds

   e number of annual visitors

   f number of pirate sailors who died

   g year the ship was discovered

   h height of rocks in metres

Writing A field trip report

1 Read the report quickly. In which paragraph (1–4) does the writer:

a give an opinion of the town and make a recommendation?

b describe the first place he/she visited in this town?

c briefly explain which town he/she visited and why he/she is writing about it?

d describe another place he/she visited in this town?

A field trip to Brighton, UK

Last summer, my class visited Brighton. ª .5. to research why Brighton is such a popular tourist destination, and to consider how it could appeal more to teenage visitors.

ᵇ .... was to the beach, which was very busy. There are several ice cream kiosks, fish and chip shops, and souvenir shops. Adventurous visitors can buy kite-surfing lessons, or pay to go on rides on Brighton Pier.

ᶜ .... we visited the town centre. We discovered many interesting clothes and music shops and other attractions, such as the beautiful, colourful Royal Pavilion. It was built over two hundred years ago, and it is visited by 400,000 people every year. However, the tickets are quite expensive for students.

ᵈ ...., we decided that Brighton was a popular tourist destination because there is so much to do there. ᵉ .... that the town could appeal more to teenagers by offering more free or cheap activities.

2 Complete the gaps (a–e) with the phrases (1–5).

1 In the afternoon
2 In conclusion
3 Our first visit
4 We also concluded
5 ~~Our aim was~~

3 Think of a city, town or village that you know well. Imagine that you visited this place on a field trip. You wanted to find out what tourists could see and do there, and to consider how the place could appeal more to teenage visitors.

Make notes.

1 What is the place and when did you go there?

....

2 Why are you writing your report?

....

3 What are *two* main attractions that you visited? (For example, *the town centre*, *the beach*, *the theme park*, *the harbour*, *the local countryside*, etc.). Give details.

First attraction:
What was it and when did you visit it?

....

What was interesting/good/bad about it?

....

Second attraction:
What was it and when did you visit it?

....

What was interesting/good/bad about it?

....

4 Can you think of one criticism of this place? (For example, *too expensive*, *not many activities*, *no interesting shops*, etc.)

....

5 How could this place appeal more to teenage visitors?

....

4 Write your field report. Use your notes from Exercise 3, and expressions from Exercises 1 and 2.

....
....
....
....
....
....
....
....
....
....

Check Your Progress 2

Grammar

1 Choose the correct options.

New Message   ⊗

Hello from New Zealand,

I ⁰*can't* believe how beautiful North Island is! You ¹.... definitely come here some time – I think you'd love it.

Yesterday we explored the Tongariro National Park where parts of the *Lord of the Rings* films ².... a few years ago. Apparently, this area ³.... by thousands of Tolkien fans every year. Some come dressed as Hobbits!

Today we ⁴.... kayaking on Lake Taupo! The kayaking trip ⁵.... at 11.00, but we ⁶.... arrive at 10.00 for a compulsory short lesson. I hope I ⁷.... too wet!

Anyway, I'd better go down to the bus, or I ⁸.... behind. Wish me luck – I ⁹.... need it! ☺

Danny

Send

0 **a** can't	**b** shouldn't	**c** mustn't
1 **a** might	**b** should	**c** will
2 **a** made	**b** are made	**c** were made
3 **a** is visited	**b** visits	**c** will visit
4 **a** should go	**b** 're going	**c** go
5 **a** might start	**b** starts	**c** is started
6 **a** mustn't	**b** could	**c** have to
7 **a** can't get	**b** won't get	**c** aren't getting
8 **a** 'll leave	**b** 'm leaving	**c** 'll be left
9 **a** might	**b** must	**c** should

/ 9 marks

2 Are these sentences correct (✓) or incorrect (✗)? Rewrite the incorrect sentences.

0 I work at the hotel next summer. ✗
I'm going to work at the hotel next summer.

1 The hut will be repaired by local builders.

....

2 I can swim when I was only four.

....

3 Watch out! You'll hit that tree!

....

4 When invented ice cream?

....

5 The next train leaves at 12.35.

....

6 You mustn't wear a hat, but it's a good idea.

....

/ 6 marks

Vocabulary

3 Choose the correct options.

0 Jess is an excellent team *communicator / (player) / worker*.

1 We visited the *amusing / amusement / amused* arcades on the pier.

2 You should *make / do / take* an appointment to see the doctor.

3 I came *down / over / across* a huge spider on the path.

4 Your work isn't *accurate / experienced / patient*. It's full of mistakes.

5 Let's walk along the sea *kiosk / wall / deck* for a while.

6 I can't work *for / on / out* the answer to this question.

/ 6 marks

4 Complete the words in bold. Write *dis-* or *re-*.

A Help! I was ⁰*re***searching** information for my Geography project, when something went wrong! All my files have ¹.......**appeared**.

B OK, keep calm! I'll see if I can ².......**store** them. There … I think I've ³.......**covered** them for you.

A Thank you, you're amazing! I really ⁴.......**like** computers sometimes …

/ 4 marks

5 Complete the descriptions of three holiday photos.

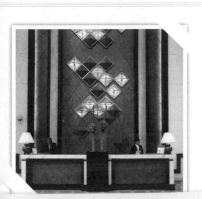

xury Hotel in Singapore
ur hotel in Singapore was
ry beautiful. This is just the
eception ¹d........................ !

Summer in Brighton
This is a photo of a brave
²s........................ standing
in front of mum's
³d........................ ! I think
he wanted our sandwiches.

osta Rican Adventure
is is Mount Arenal,
⁴v........................ . We
w it ⁵e........................ with
moke, rocks and fire!

Speaking

6 Choose the correct options.

A Hello. Willoughby College.

B Oh hello. I'm ⁰*asking /* (*calling*) */ ringing* about Jed Kane's photography class. I ¹*would / like / 'd like* to book a place, please.

A I'm afraid it won't be possible to attend a class with Jed.

B Sorry, I don't ²*know / understand / see*. Are you ³*saying / speaking / telling* that the course is cancelled?

A No, but Mel Wyatt now runs the class instead. The next class starts tonight, in the Main Hall.

B Oh, I ⁴*see / look / watch*! Could you book me a place with Mel, please? And could you tell me how I ⁵*direct / get / go* to the Main Hall from Green Street?

A Turn left and go ⁶*along / pass / past* the library. ⁷*Go / Take / Turn* the second turning on the right. The college is ⁸*at / by / on* the left. You can't miss it!

B Thanks!

A I'll just ⁹*pass / give / put* you over to our Education Officer. She'll take your details. ¹⁰*Give / Hold / Wait* on please …

Translation

7 Translate the sentences.

1 The house was buried by the avalanche.

....

2 I'm going to write a report about the harbour.

....

3 We must keep on walking or we might not survive.

....

4 The old ice cream kiosk will be restored next year.

....

5 Many animals couldn't swim so they drowned in the flood.

....

Dictation

8 🔊 21   Listen and write.

1 ....
2 ....
3 ....
4 ....
5 ....

7 Final Frontiers

Vocabulary Adjective antonyms

★ **1** Choose the correct antonym for the adjectives in bold.

1 **temporary**: permanent / powerful / wide
2 **high**: wide / low / shallow
3 **weak**: dark / high / powerful
4 **wide**: ordinary / narrow / strong
5 **modern**: ancient / deep / permanent
6 **light**: narrow / strange / dark
7 **shallow**: deep / wide / heavy
8 **ordinary**: temporary / ancient / strange

★ **2** Complete the sentences. Use the antonym of the adjectives in bold.

ancient	high	light	narrow
permanent	shallow	strange	strong

1 It's only a **low** hill. We'll climb it easily.
It's a *high* mountain. We can't climb it in one day.

2 This place seems very **ordinary**. I'm bored!
This place is quite .... It's fascinating!

3 These bags are **heavy**. Can you carry one?
These bags are .... I can carry one more.

4 This **modern** tower was built last year.
This .... tower was built in 789!

5 This river is **deep**. We'll have to swim across.
This river is .... We can walk across.

6 This sick horse is very **weak**. She can't stand up.
This horse is very .... She can carry heavy weights.

7 This is their **temporary** home. They're going to move soon.
This is their .... home. They've lived here their whole lives.

8 Lots of traffic travels through the **wide** streets.
No traffic can travel down the .... streets.

Vocabulary page 110

★★ **3** Complete the sentences with these adjectives. There are two adjectives you do not need.

ancient	deep	high	low
~~modern~~	narrow	shallow	wide

Tokyo, **Japan**, is a very ¹*modern city*. Most buildings there are less than a hundred years old. Many skyscrapers in Tokyo are very ² .... – the tallest is 634 metres. Tokyo is on the Sumida River, which flows into the sea in Tokyo Bay. The river is quite ³ .... and is crossed by many long bridges.

TOKYO

Damascus, **Syria**, is very ⁴ .... People lived here almost 12,000 years ago! The oldest buildings here have sunk over time, so they're quite ⁵ .... Some are below the ground. The Barada river flows through the city. Damascus is in a very dry area, so the river is very ⁶ .... , with very little water.

DAMASCUS

★★ **4** Rewrite the sentences. Use an antonym of the adjectives in bold. Change the verbs.

1 The building is **ancient**.
The building *isn't modern*.
2 The lake isn't **deep**.
The lake ....
3 The water was **low**.
The water ....
4 He didn't look **strong**.
He ....
5 It's our temporary **home**.
It ....
6 They lived on a **narrow** street.
They ....

Reading

★ **1** Read the newspaper article quickly. Tick (✓) the animals which definitely exist today.

1 Bigfoot
2 Mountain gorilla
3 Mokele-mbembe
4 Tasmanian tiger
5 Hippo
6 Giant squid

★ **2** Read the article again and complete the information sheet.

The Mokele-mbembe

Appearance: It looks like a ¹*dinosaur*.
Its colour is ²........................ .

Habitat: It lives in ³........................ and
⁴........................ in the Congo.

Food: It eats: ⁵........................

★ **3** Choose the best options.

1 What evidence is there for Mokele-mbembes?
a films b photos ⓒ stories

2 What does the writer tell us about scientists?
a They were surprised when explorers discovered a Mokele-mbembe.
b Some local people disagree with them about the Mokele-mbembe.
c None believe that Mokele-mbembes really exist.

3 Why do local people think it will be difficult to photograph a Mokele-mbembe?
a They aren't easy to see.
b They never leave the water.
c They are dangerous.

4 What do we learn about the explorers' journey this year?
a They are taking their own food.
b The trip may last more than three months.
c No one has made this journey before.

5 How many different kinds of animals do we definitely know about today?
a less than 5,000
b over 1 million
c over 8 million

6 What do we learn about recent animal discoveries?
a Big animal discoveries never happen.
b 19,000 new insects were discovered last year.
c Most new animal discoveries are insects.

★★ **4** Based on evidence from this article, how likely do you think it is that the explorers will find a Mokele-mbembe?

impossible / quite unlikely / very likely / certain

Explorers hunt for African dinosaur

Explorers are going to the Congo to try to find Mokele-mbembes, strange animals which look like dinosaurs.

There are many stories about dinosaurs living in deep rivers and lakes in modern Congo. However, no one has ever filmed a Mokele-mbembe, and there are no clear, convincing photos. If the explorers found new evidence, many scientists would be very surprised. Most think that, like 'Bigfoot' in North America, Mokele-mbembes don't exist! However, some local people say that they've seen the animals themselves.

Nevertheless, finding a Mokele-mbembe won't be easy. According to traditional Congo stories, they live mainly in water and they don't often leave it. They're the same colour as their environment – grey. If one noticed the explorers, it wouldn't attack them, because this peaceful animal is thought to eat only plants. But the explorers need to watch out for hippos and crocodiles – which are very real, and very dangerous!

Other explorers have tried the same journey and failed. Some local people now believe that the last Mokele-mbembes have died, like Tasmanian tigers and other extinct animals. But this year's explorers say they feel hopeful. They are going to travel for three months. If they stay any longer, they'll run out of food!

Although their chances of finding a Mokele-mbembe seem small, the explorers may come across other interesting animals. So far we know about 1.3 million kinds of animals worldwide, including more than 5,400 mammals*. However, there might be as many as 8.7 million animals in total. Last year, around 19,000 new kinds of plants and animals were discovered – mostly insects. 'Big animal' discoveries are unusual, but not impossible. Until 1902, few people knew about mountain gorillas. The first live giant squid was photographed in 2002! And the Mkole-mbembe? Well, if the explorers find anything, we'll let you know!

* mammal = animal with warm blood and a backbone.
For example, monkeys, bears and humans.

Grammar First and Second conditional

★ **1a** Match the sentence beginnings (1–6) to the endings (a–f) to make conditional sentences.

1 If I discovered a new country, *c*
2 If it's sunny tomorrow,
3 If I won the lottery,
4 If there's nothing good on TV tonight,
5 If I was the teacher,
6 If I don't get a job,

a I'd buy my own island.
b I won't have much money.
c I'd name it after myself!
d I wouldn't give my students any homework!
e I won't watch it.
f I'll walk to school.

b Look at the sentences again. Which ones are true for you?

★ **2** Choose the correct options. Are these situations likely (*L*) or unlikely (*U*) to happen?

The future of the planet?

1 The world (would be)/ is a greener place if we stopped driving cars. *U*
2 If the planet *continues / would continue* to get hotter, sea levels will get higher.
3 We wouldn't have as many famines if droughts *don't exist / didn't exist.*
4 If scientists explore the sea, they *'ll discover / 'd discover* new fish and plants.
5 What *will happen / would happen* if we discovered alien life in space?
6 Some animals *won't survive / wouldn't survive* if we don't help the environment.
7 If we *destroyed / destroy* more forests, what will happen to the planet?

★★ **3** Complete the text with the correct form of the verbs. Use the First or Second conditional.

URBAN EXPLORER BLOG

THURSDAY, MARCH 14

Hi! I'm Max, and I'm an urban explorer. If it ¹ *doesn't rain* (not rain) tomorrow, I'll climb some of the highest buildings in my town! I ² .... (take) some photos from the top if I see anything interesting. I usually do! If I ³ .... (not climb), I wouldn't see so many strange and amazing sights. Cities are beautiful from above. If you climbed with me, you ⁴ .... (understand). I ⁵ .... (not explore) a building if I don't think it's safe. I'm always really careful. If I ⁶ .... (fall), I would get really hurt. Luckily, I'm not scared of heights. If I was, this hobby ⁷ .... (not be) much fun!

If you ⁸ .... (search) for 'urban exploring' online, you'll be able to find out more. There are some great photos!

★★ **4** Are these events or situations possible or unlikely? Write a First or Second conditional sentence.

1 (become rich and famous / buy a yacht)
If *I became rich and famous, I'd buy a yacht.*
2 (travel into space / visit different planets)
If ....
3 (get better at English / do more practice)
I ....
4 (be extremely wealthy / not do any work)
If ....
5 (have lots of free time / not have any homework next year)
I ....
6 (not stay at home all day / it / be sunny this weekend)
I ....
7 (not get any answers right in this exercise / be disappointed)
If ....

Grammar Reference pages 98–99

Vocabulary Space

1 Complete the descriptions of jobs with these words.

astronaut	~~astronomer~~
solar	spacecraft
stars	telescope

A An ¹*astronomer* uses a
²........................ to look at
³........................ and planets in
the night sky.

B An ⁴........................ travels in a
⁵........................ to explore the
⁶........................ system.

2 Complete the crossword with space words.

Down

1 something that looks like a bright star with a tail
3 a large group of stars
4 a big object which moves round the Earth and which was visited by Neil Armstrong

Across

2 a planet's journey round the Sun
5 a kind of very small planet
6 for example: Earth, Mars, or Venus
7 there are eight planets in our *solar* …

3 Complete the space timeline with these words. Which fact do you think is the most interesting?

asteroid	astronaut	astronomer	galaxy	orbit
planet	spacecraft	~~stars~~	system	telescope

Space exploration and discovery

c. 400BC Democritus suggests that a light shape in the night sky might be a group of ¹*stars* (now called a ²........................).

1543 Nicolaus Copernicus developed the first idea of the solar ³........................ . Before then, most people believed that the Sun moved in an ⁴........................ around the Earth.

1608 The first ⁵........................s for looking at stars were invented by men who made reading glasses.

1609 The famous ⁶........................ Galileo Galilei first used a telescope.

1781 The seventh ⁷........................ , Uranus, was discovered. It is made of ice and gas.

1801 When the first ⁸........................ was discovered, scientists thought it was a small planet.

1957 The first ⁹........................ from Earth travelled into space. No one was inside it.

1963 The first female ¹⁰........................ in space was Valentina Tereshkova, two years after Yuri Gagarin.

4 Look at the photo. Then complete the text. Write one space word in each gap.

This photo shows lots of ¹*stars*, as well as a bright
²........................ with a long tail. The photo also shows the
Earth's ³........................ , which completes its ⁴........................
around our planet in around 27.3 days. There are eight
⁵........................ in our ⁶........................ system.
⁷........................ , who study space, have discovered that six
of them (Earth, Mars, Jupiter, Saturn, Uranus and Neptune)
have their own moons.

Chatroom — Giving warnings

Speaking and Listening

★ 1 🔊 22 **Match the statements (1–6) with the warnings (a–f) to make conversations. Then listen and check.**

1 I'm going to stay here for another five minutes. *c*
2 I'm going to order a pizza.
3 I'm going to deliver this newspaper next door.
4 I'm going to buy her some flowers.
5 I'm going to walk by the river.
6 I'm going to go to bed.

a Make sure you don't get roses. She hates them!
b Watch out for the mosquitoes! They love water.
c Be careful not to miss the bus!
d Be careful not to wake your little brother.
e Watch out for their horrible dog!
f I wouldn't order the pepperoni one if I were you. It's hot!

Brain Trainer

Write complete sentences to help you to remember how to use everyday expressions.

Do Exercise 2. Then copy one example sentence for each 'warning' expression into your vocabulary notebook.

★★ 2 **Complete the conversations with these words and phrases.**

Be careful   Make   ~~Watch~~   Watch   were   wouldn't

1 A I'm going to eat in the garden.
   B *Watch* out for the insects!
2 A I'm going to do my homework in front of the TV.
   B .... not to make mistakes!
3 A I'm going to walk on the cliff.
   B .... out for the wet rocks!
4 A I'm going to go to the beach.
   B .... sure you don't forget your sunscreen. It's hot!
5 A I'm going to go to the cinema.
   B I .... watch the new horror film if I .... you. It's terrible!

★★ 3 🔊 23 **Listen to the conversation about Polly's holiday. Put the activities in the correct order. There is one activity you don't need.**

a mountain biking   ....
b meeting friends   ....
c horse riding   ....
d kayaking   *.1.*
e caving   ....

★★ 4 🔊 23 **Listen again. Complete the five warnings you hear.**

1 Watch *out for the crocodiles*!
2 W... ....
   ....!
3 Be c......................... ....
   .... too fast!
4 Make s......................... ....
   .... lost!
5 I wouldn't g......................... ....
   if I ....

★★ 5 **Do you think that Liam would like to go on Polly's holiday?**
Yes / No / We don't know

★★ 6 **Imagine that different friends tell you they are going to do activities 1–4. You give them all warnings. Write short conversations, using different warning phrases.**

1 go for a walk (warning: alone)
   A *I'm going to go for a walk.*
   B *OK, but I wouldn't go alone if I were you. You might get lost! I'll go with you.*
2 swim in the sea (warning: jellyfish)
3 try skateboarding (warning: fall)
4 have a first driving lesson (warning: crash)

Speaking and Listening page 119

Grammar Subject/Object questions

Brain Trainer

Try saying questions out loud as well as reading and writing them. It will help you to remember how to form them correctly.

Do Exercise 1. Then say the questions out loud.

★ 1a Write *S* for a subject question and *O* for an object question.

The A, B, C of countries

A Which country did Captain James Cook sail to?   .O.
Answer: Australia

B Where does the biggest rainforest grow?   ....
Answer: B........................

C Which country invented paper, fireworks and sunglasses?   ....
Answer: C........................

D Where do people make LEGO®?   ....
Answer: D........................

E Who built the Pyramids?   ....
Answer: people from E........................

F What shares borders with Belgium, Switzerland, Italy and Spain?   ....
Answer: F........................

b Guess the countries.

★ 2 Complete the Past simple questions.

1 *Which famous Italian explorer thought*
Which famous Italian explorer / think that the Earth was flat? Christopher Columbus!

2 ....
When / Columbus / become a sailor? When he was a teenager.

3 ....
What / the young Columbus / sell? Maps.

4 ....
Who / give / Columbus the money for his ships? Queen Isabella and King Ferdinand of Spain.

5 ....
Who / Columbus / take with him on his fourth journey to South America? His son, Ferdinand.

6 ....
Which Europeans / travel to North America first? Scandinavians.

★★ 3 Write Present simple and Past simple questions. Answer the questions so they are true for you.

1 Who / you / live / with / ?
Who do you live with?

2 Where / your family / go on holiday / last year / ?
....

3 Who / speak / to you first / today / ?
....

4 What / usually / happen / on your birthday / ?
....

5 Which people / inspire / you / today?
....

6 Which places / you / want to explore / in the future / ?
....

7 What fact or story / interest / you / the most / in Unit 7 / ?
....

★★ 4 Write subject or object questions with *Who* or *What* for the missing information. Then choose the correct options.

1 *Who did a Hawaiian man kill while he was repairing his boats in 1779?*
A Hawaiian man killed .... while he was repairing his boats in 1779.
ⓐ James Cook   **b** John Cabot
c Hernán Cortés

2 ....?
Spanish explorers brought back .... , potatoes and chocolate from Mexico in the 1500s.
a tomatoes   **b** carrots   **c** cucumbers

3 ....?
.... led the first round-the-world expedition.
a da Gama   **b** Columbus   **c** Magellan

4 ....?
A NASA spacecraft found .... on Mars.
a plants   **b** ice   **c** oil

5 ....?
HMS Beagle took .... to South America and Australia.
a Roald Amundsen   **b** Francis Drake
c Charles Darwin

6 .... in 2003?
.... ate American naturalist Timothy Treadwell in 2003.
a A crocodile   **b** A bear   **c** A lion

Grammar Reference pages 98– 99

Reading

1 Read the interview quickly. Choose the best heading.

   a A new kind of tourism
   b New spacecraft technologies
   c How to be an astronaut

2 Complete the interview. Complete the gaps (1–6) with the questions (a–f).

   a How much do space trips cost?
   b What is space tourism?
   c What will spacecraft be like in the future?
   d Has anyone tried it before?
   e Is space travel safe?
   f So space travel is only for really wealthy people?

3 According to the interview, what are the two main disadvantages of space travel at the moment? Write two adjectives.

It's very .... and it might be
....

Listening

1 🔊 **24** Listen to an interviewer asking people the same question. Then answer the questions.

   1 Complete the question: 'How will life be different in .... ?'
   2 How many different people answer the interviewer's question? ....

2 🔊 **24** Listen again. Choose the correct options to complete the predictions.

   1 I think we will discover new *planets* / *animals*.
   2 If we travel to new galaxies, maybe we'll find *aliens* / *new places to live*.
   3 Pollution will get *worse* / *better*.
   4 Illnesses will be a *bigger* / *smaller* problem.
   5 The worst problem will be *droughts* / *floods*.
   6 *Scientists* / *Politicians* will save the world.

3a Are most speakers generally positive or negative about the future?

....

  b What's *your* attitude to the future? Which predictions do you agree with?

Many of us dream of going into space. Now, according to space expert Idris Shah, some of us can make our dreams come true. We asked him for details.

Q ¹ .b.

A It's just that – travelling into space for pleasure. You'll be able to see amazing views of Earth, or try fun space experiments!

Q ² ....

A Oh yes, this isn't a new idea. The American businessman Dennis Tito was the first 'space guest' in 2001. He spent eight days in orbit above the Earth.

Q ³ ....

A Millions! No one knows exactly how much Tito paid, but some people think it was around $20 million. Unfortunately, if you buy a ticket now, it will be even more expensive! A British company is currently selling places on a space flight for around £200 million.

Q ⁴ ....

A At the moment, yes. If I won the lottery tomorrow, I still wouldn't be able to afford that price! But in a few years' time, things will be different. When people started sailing around the world in the fifteenth to the seventeenth centuries, big sea voyages were new, strange and extremely expensive. Now, they're quite ordinary, and good value.

Q ⁵ ....

A Well, if you ask me, the next big invention will be 'space trains'. One team estimates these will be possible in only twenty years. Trains will be able to carry more people, so tickets will be cheaper – about $5,000.

Q ⁶ ....

A Well, there are dangers, but that's true for other leisure activities, like diving or caving. Of course, there aren't any emergency rescue services in space! That's why all space travel companies teach passengers how to be astronauts *before* they fly. You need to know what to do if things go wrong.

Writing An application letter

1 Read the advertisement and the application letter quickly. Do you think Alyssa is likely or unlikely to have an interview with the company? Would you like to do this job?

....

Temporary summer vacancies

We're looking for teenage volunteers to join our summer programme! With support and training, you will help us to answer questions from our many international visitors, and give fun science presentations. An interest in space or science is essential, and knowledge of some foreign languages would be an advantage.

---

¹ Hi / (Dear) Sir/Madam,

Teenage volunteers

I was very ² *interested* / *interesting* to see your advert for temporary summer vacancies on your website. I ³ *am writing* / *write* to apply for a job as a teenage volunteer at the Space Centre.

I have always been interested in the stars, and for many years it has been my dream to study astronomy at university. ⁴ *If* / *When* I worked at the Space Centre, it would be excellent experience for my future career.

I would be a hardworking and enthusiastic member of the team. Science is my strongest school subject, and I ⁵ *could* / *can* speak English, Spanish and French. I am a good communicator, and I have experience of teaching chess at school. I have never worked in a museum, but I learn new skills quickly.

I very much ⁶ *hope* / *want* that you will choose me as a volunteer. I look forward to ⁷ *hear* / *hearing* from you.

⁸ *Yours* / *Your* faithfully,

Alyssa Douglas

Alyssa Douglas

2 Choose the correct options to complete Alyssa's letter.

3 Read the advert below and decide which tour you'd prefer to work on. Then write notes in the paragraph plan.

EXPLORE SOUTH AMERICA

Volunteer opportunities for trainee tour guides

We're looking for volunteers to work on our popular tours for young international tourists: the 'Nature and History Tour' (Peru), which takes us up high mountains to the ancient city of Machu Picchu; and the 'Space Tour' (Chile), where we will explore the Atacama desert and view stars through the famous Alma telescope.

Tour guides: You will answer questions and help us to keep guests happy! Knowledge of one or more foreign languages is essential. Please say which tour you would prefer to work on and why.

Paragraph 1: Say why you're writing. (Which tour do you prefer?)

....
....

Paragraph 2: Say why you want the job. (What are your interests?)

....
....

Paragraph 3: Say why you would be a good trainee tour guide. (Have you got any useful skills or experience?)

....
....

Paragraph 4: Say what you would like to happen next. (I hope … I look forward …)

....
....

4 Write your application letter. Use the correct layout and language for a formal letter. Include your ideas from Exercise 3.

....
....
....
....
....
....
....
....
....

8 Spies

Vocabulary Spy collocations

★ **1** Complete the spy collocations in sentences 1–6. Each letter of the missing words matches one symbol (●, ♦, ♣, etc.) in the code. Solve the code to discover the secret word.

1 We <u>f o l l o w</u> (✱✚☎☎✚➲) someone when we want to spy on them.

2 We tell _ _ _ _ (☎▲□◇) when we want people to believe things that aren't true.

3 The police might tap a _ _ _ _ _ (♣★✚➺□) to secretly listen to a conversation.

4 Someone wears a _ _ _ _ _ _ _ _ (♣▲◇⊗♥▲◇□) when they don't want to be recognised.

5 Honest people tell the _ _ _ _ _ (❯✖♥❯★).

6 We _ _ _ _ _ _ (♣□♦✚♣□) a secret _ _ _ _ _ _ _ (♣□◇◇●⊗□) that is difficult to understand.

Code

◈	●	♠	■	❖	♦	➲	♣	☾	□	♥	✱	❯
z		y	b	x		w		v			f	

⊗	◇	★	✖	▲	➡	✪	❖	✏	✚	☎	➺	✿
					q	j			k	o	l	

What's the secret word? ....
(♦✖▲✿▲➺●☎)

⚙ **Brain Trainer**

Remember: some verbs have two parts *work + out; look + after*.

Record and revise both parts of the phrasal verb.

Do Exercise 2. Which phrasal verbs can you find?

★ **2** Match the sentence beginnings (1–6) with the endings (a–f).

1 The prisoner Mal made   *e*
2 They helped Mal to escape
3 Mal broke
4 Eloise tracked
5 She took
6 She spied on

a Mal down to the house.
b cover in the park and watched him.
c from the prison.
d Mal at the house, then arrested him.
e a deal with other prisoners.
f into an empty house to hide.

★★ **3** Complete the text about a famous character with the correct form of suitable crime words. Who is it?

This fictional detective knew almost immediately if someone was telling [1]l*ies* or telling the [2]t...................... . He didn't [3]t...................... people's phones, because the technology didn't exist in the nineteenth century. However, he [4]d...................... many secret messages very quickly. When he was [5]f...................... people around London in order to [6]s...................... on them, he wore many [7]d...................... , including the clothes of an old sailor, a priest, and a woman! However, on TV he is perhaps most famous for his unusual hat.

Famous character: ....

Vocabulary page 111

Reading

Brain Trainer

Read the title of a text and look at any photos before you read the whole text. Do the title and photos give you any clues about the topic? What do you already know about this topic?

Now do Exercise 1.

★ **1a** Read the title of the profile and look at the photo. Can you guess the answers to questions 1–5? What else do you know?

1 What was James Bond's code name? _007_
2 Who wrote the James Bond stories? ....
3 What nationality was this writer? ....
4 Which film actor first played James Bond?
....
5 Name a famous Bond enemy with an unusual hat.
....

b Read the whole profile quickly to check your answers.

★ **2** Read the profile again and write the dates.

1 ...._1908_....... Ian Fleming was born.
2 .... Ian Fleming's war work ended.
3 .... Ian Fleming moved to Jamaica.
4 .... James Bond was created.
5 .... The first Bond film was made.
6 .... Ian Fleming died.

★ **3** Complete the sentences using information from the text. Write between two and four words in each gap.

1 As well as writing articles and books, Ian Fleming used to work on _secret military projects_.
2 As well as a military project, 'Golden Eye' was the name of a film and ....
3 James Bond was named after ....
4 .... is one hobby that Fleming and his fictional hero both share.
5 As well as silver sports cars, Bond has also driven ....
6 The most recent films aren't based on books by Fleming, because Fleming .... novels!

★ **4** According to the writer of this profile, tick (✓) the two descriptions that best match Bond. Is her general attitude more positive or critical?

adventurous ☐　　boring ☐　　enjoys jokes ☐
sensible ☐　　likeable ☐　　ordinary ☐

Julia's attitude is more .... than
....

online *profiles*

The name's Bond, James Bond

Profile by Julia Hawkhead

👍 Like

The spy with the code name 007 was 'born' in 1952. He was created by Ian Fleming, a writer and journalist who'd worked on a number of secret military projects from 1939–1945, including one to track down the German 'Enigma' machine, which was used for coding and decoding messages in World War Two. Another project was called 'Golden Eye', which later became the name of a Bond film – and Fleming's house. Like his fictional hero, Fleming was also fond of jokes.

Ian Fleming was born in England in 1908, but he wrote the 'Bond' novels in Jamaica, where he'd lived since 1945. His cold-hearted but handsome hero wasn't named after a war spy, but a local bird expert (Fleming was a keen birdwatcher). Fleming said that he wanted an ordinary name, because that's what he thought Bond was like. Perhaps this was another joke, because everyone else would disagree!

Bond isn't always easy to like, but he's a long way from boring. It's true that, just like his creator, his favourite sport is golf. But we can forgive that, because he also loves danger, adventure, and following villains in fast cars. Although he's most famous for driving a silver Aston Martin, he also takes the wheel of a large bus in *Live and Let Die*! Bond and his enemies may not always make sensible decisions, but they show great imagination in choosing weapons. In *From Russia With Love*, Bond uses an exploding briefcase. In *Goldfinger*, the evil Oddjob kills people with his hat!

Fleming's fascinating spy has appeared in more than fifty years of Bond films, with Sean Connery first playing the role in 1962. But Fleming had only written twelve Bond novels before he died in 1964. The latest 'Bond' adventures are now written by new authors and screenwriters. Is 007 the spy who lives forever?

Grammar Past perfect

★ 1 Complete the web article. Use the Past perfect.

→ In Oregon, USA, a thief felt tired after he
¹ 'd entered (enter) a stranger's home to steal.
By the time the home owner returned, the
burglar ² .... (fall) asleep!

→ After he ³ .... (damage) a building,
a British teenager wrote 'Peter Addison was
here' on the wall! The police found Peter after
they ⁴ .... (search) for his name
on their computers.

→ The police arrived after two burglars
⁵ .... (already/leave) a crime scene
in Iowa, USA. But the thieves were easy to find,
because they ⁶ .... (not choose) very
good disguises. They ⁷ .... (draw)
on their faces using black pens!

★ 2 Choose the correct verb forms to complete
the newspaper report.

Ellie Good ¹ *just stopped / had just stopped* to speak to
a friend in town when her little dog 'Coco' ² *saw /
had seen* a cat. Before Ellie realised what was happening,
Coco ³ *escaped / had escaped* from her lead and was
running towards a busy road! A terrified Ellie called for
help – and Spiderman appeared! Josh Hearn, who ⁴ *dressed /
'd dressed* as Spiderman for a party, was walking past when
he heard Ellie's call. Josh ⁵ *caught / had caught* Coco before
she ⁶ *crossed / 'd crossed* the road. Ellie was delighted.
'Forget Spiderman – Josh is my hero,' she said.

★★ 3 Complete the text with the correct Past
perfect or Past simple form of these verbs.

already/leave	~~be~~	be	close
go	put	just/steal	track

On the morning of 22 August, 1911, art gallery
staff at the Louvre ¹ *were* shocked to discover that
someone ² .... the famous Mona Lisa
painting! By this time the thief, Vincenzo Peruggia,
³ .... Paris.

Before the museum ⁴ .... the day
before, Vincenzo Peruggia had hidden inside the
building. After everyone ⁵ .... home,
he cut down the painting. After that, he simply
walked out. No one noticed anything unusual
about Peruggia, because he ⁶ .... the
painting under his shirt!

By the time the police eventually ⁷ ....
Peruggia down, the painting ⁸ ....
missing for two years.

★★ 4 Write one sentence for each situation. Use the
Past perfect or the Past simple and the time
expressions.

1 She followed the thief home. Then she took
cover in his garden. (after)
*After she'd followed the thief home, she took
cover in his garden.*

2 He went to the police. They made a deal. (after)
....
....

3 They tracked us down. It was some time before
2 o'clock. (by 2 o'clock)
....
....

4 Immediately after she found the address, she
heard a call for help. (just)
She ....
when ....

5 He decoded the secret message and then he
burnt it. (before)
He ....
....

6 The criminal escaped. Then the detective
arrived. (already)
By the time ....
....

Grammar Reference pages 100–101

Vocabulary Adjectives with prefixes *dis-*, *im-*, *in-*, *un-*

★ **1** Choose the correct negative prefix.

1 (in-) / un- / dis- correct
2 un- / im- / in- fair
3 im- / dis- / in- satisfied
4 dis- / un- / im- possible
5 in- / dis- / un- important
6 un- / in- / im- appropriate

★ **2** Phil is the opposite of Sarah. Complete the sentences about Phil. Add prefixes to the adjectives in bold.

1 Sara is **polite** and friendly to everyone. Phil is *impolite* and unfriendly to people he doesn't like.
2 Sara is very **patient**. She doesn't mind waiting. Phil is very .... He hates waiting.
3 Sara is an **honest** person who tells the truth. Phil is a .... person who tells lies!
4 Sara is **successful** at school and work. Phil is .... at school and work.
5 Sara is very **tolerant** of different kinds of people. Phil is very .... He wants everyone to be just like him!
6 Sara is **loyal** to her friends. You can rely on her. Phil is .... to his friends. You can't trust him!

★ **3** Complete the adjectives. There is one adjective you do not need.

| appropriate | fair | ~~honest~~ | loyal |
| patient | possible | successful | |

In the 1960s, the CIA tried to train 'spy cats'. No, I'm not being [1] dis*honest* – this really happened! 'Spy training' was so difficult it was almost [2] im........................! Cats don't like rules, and they're [3] im........................ of waiting. Also, cats can be [4] dis........................ , unlike dogs, which are famous for their loyalty! Some people think it's [5] in........................ to use cats as spies, especially as they can't speak for themselves. Sadly, the experiment was [6] un........................ , as the first spy cat was run over by a taxi on its first mission.

★★ **4a** Complete the sentences. Use a prefix and these adjectives. There are two adjectives you do not need.

| appropriate | correct | fair | important |
| loyal | ~~polite~~ | possible | satisfied |

1 Please show more respect! It's very *impolite* to listen to other people's conversations.
2 I never get to follow the most interesting suspects, but 008 always does! It's so ....!
3 These disguises are .... for night work. Everyone will notice us in bright yellow!
4 I can't believe you tapped our phones. You're so .... to your friends.
5 It was .... to take cover in his garden, because there were no trees or walls.
6 Never read my diary again! Luckily, I only write about .... things there, like music and jokes, so you were probably quite disappointed.

b Which of the statements (1–6) were said:

• by a spy?   ....
• to a spy?   ....

★★ **5** Agree with these statements. Use an adjective with a negative prefix that has a similar meaning to the underlined words.

1 A Wearing the 'right' clothes <u>doesn't matter</u>.
  B I agree. It's completely *unimportant*.
2 A I'm afraid he <u>often tells lies</u>.
  B I know. He's very ....
3 A She <u>hates waiting</u>, doesn't she?
  B Oh yes. She's very ....!
4 A These answers are <u>wrong</u>.
  B I agree. They're all ....!
5 A He <u>never achieved anything</u> in life.
  B I know. It's sad, but he was always ....
6 A He <u>definitely can't be</u> a spy!
  B Of course not! It's completely ....!
7 A He <u>won't accept any opinions which are different from his own</u>.
  B I agree! He's so ....

Speaking and Listening

★ 1 🔊 **25** **Look at the picture and answer the questions. Then listen and check. Were you right?**

1 Who do you think the bag belongs to? ....

2 What do you think the boy might be looking for? ....

★ 2 🔊 **25** **Listen again and complete the dialogue. Write one word in each gap.**

A Hey! What's ¹*going* on? Why are you looking in my bag?

B Oh, hi there. I'm just looking for a ² ....

A Well, you should ask me first. My bag is private.

B I ³ .... that. But the ⁴ .... is that you weren't here, and I really need to finish this exercise before the next class.

A I'm sure that's ⁵ .... You never do your homework on time! But you shouldn't take other people's stuff without asking.

B I know. I'm ⁶ .... that I upset you.

A Oh, let's ⁷ .... about it. Here – you can borrow this one. But please give it back!

★★ 3 **Choose the best options to complete the conversations.**

A The ¹*fact*/ *information* is that you weren't here.

B I'm aware ² *about / of* that. But you should never look at people's private stuff!

A I ³ *agree / know* that. Sorry.

A I'm ⁴ *afraid / sorry* that I upset you.

B OK, well, let's forget ⁵ *about / of* it.

A You have to ⁶ *think / understand* that it was a mistake.

B I'm ⁷ *aware / sure* that's true.

★★ 4 🔊 **26** **Listen to the conversation. Then answer the questions.**

1 Where are the speakers? *in town*

2 What is the relationship between the two speakers? (For example: *teacher and student*.) ....

3 Where did the female speaker think the male speaker was going? ....

4 Where was he *really* going and *why*? .... because ....

5 Who apologises? ....

6 Does the conversation end positively or unhappily? ....

★★ 5a 🔊 **26** **Listen again and correct the mistakes in the expressions. There may be more than one mistake.**

1 You must to understand that I was worried. *You have to understand that I was worried.*   *E*

2 I'm aware about that! ....

3 I'm sure that's truth. ....

4 It is the fact that I wanted to buy you a present. ....

5 I'm sorry for I followed you. ....

6 Let we forgetting about it. ....

b **Are these expressions for explaining (*E*), acknowledging (*A*), or apologising/accepting an apology (*AP*)?**

★★ 6 **Imagine that you find your friend looking at your English notebook without asking. Think of a reason for his/her behaviour (for example: he/she didn't understand something in class). Write a short conversation. Include phrases for explaining, acknowledging, apologising and accepting an apology.**

You Sara. Why are you looking at my English notes?

Sara ....

Speaking and Listening page 120

Grammar Third conditional

★ **1** Choose the endings which are *not* correct for the sentence beginnings (1–6).

1 Would you have known …
   (a) if you didn't spy on them?
   b if they'd lied to you?
   c if I hadn't told you?

2 If they hadn't made a deal, …
   a he wouldn't have apologised.
   b she won't help them.
   c I'd have been surprised.

3 The spy wouldn't have seen him, …
   a if she'd looked the other way.
   b if he hadn't made a noise.
   c if we helped him to escape.

4 If you'd seen the crime, …
   a will you report it?
   b what would you have done?
   c would you have run away?

5 Where would he have gone …
   a if he'd reached the airport?
   b if the police didn't catch him?
   c if we'd given him the car keys?

6 If you hadn't been so dishonest, …
   a she had already forgiven you.
   b we would have stayed friends.
   c this wouldn't have happened.

★ **2** Complete the Third conditional sentences with the correct form of the verbs.

TICLE

The Graff Robbery

On 6 August 2009, some men went to the luxury Graff Jewellery store in London. The door assistant ¹ *wouldn't have let* (not let) them in if they ² .... (not be) so well-dressed and polite. If the assistant ³ .... (ask) them to leave, they ⁴ .... (not take) jewellery worth nearly £40 million! Luckily for the police, while the robbers were escaping, one man dropped his mobile phone. If the police ⁵ .... (not find) the mobile phone, they ⁶ .... (not track) down the thieves so quickly. The police ⁷ .... (return) the jewels to the store if the thieves ⁸ .... (tell) them where to look. But the jewels haven't been found … yet!

★★ **3** Rewrite the sentences using the Third conditional.

1 Desi went into town because he wanted to meet friends.
   If Desi hadn't wanted to meet friends, he *wouldn't have gone into town.*

2 Desi didn't take the bus because he didn't have enough money.
   If .... ,
   Desi ....

3 When he walked down Green Street, he heard Millie shout 'help'.
   He ....
   if ....

4 Desi ran because he saw a thief taking Millie's bag.
   If .... ,
   Desi ....

★★ **4** Write sentences with the Third conditional to show how things could have been different. Use all the ideas in the story chain.

not hear loud noise → stay asleep → not go downstairs → not see thief → not phone police → they not catch thief → she steal our ???

1 *If I hadn't heard a loud noise, I would have stayed asleep.*
2 *If I'd stayed asleep,* ....
3 ....
4 ....
5 ....
6 ....

Grammar Reference pages 100–101

Reading

1 Read the debate quickly. Who is for the idea in the introduction and who is against it?

1 For: ....

2 Against: ....

Student spies

In several American schools, some students spy on other students and report any serious problems to teachers or the police. In return, they receive rewards, like clothes or money. Is this a good idea? Two British students give their views.

Ellie

A few months ago, someone stole my mobile phone after I'd left my bag in the classroom. In the end, the girl who had taken it felt so bad that she returned it. She was in a lot of trouble, but the school allowed her to stay because she'd told the truth and apologised. But if she'd been reported by a 'spy' first, the school would probably have asked her to leave straightaway. In a school of spies, no one would trust anyone. Some students might even tell lies about people they don't like, especially if they think they'll get some money! I agree that crime can be a problem. However, instead of training 'spies', I think we need more school counselling programmes to help students instead.

Finn

Schools aren't safe. Last year, there were 65 serious attacks in schools *every day*! Some older students used to make my little brother very unhappy. If teachers had known what was happening, they would have stopped it. But my brother was too frightened to tell anyone. In the end, he went to hospital after the older boys had hurt him in a fight! The police arrested his attackers and my brother is OK now, but it was a terrifying time. Teachers can't see everything that's going on. Maybe, if the school had had student spies, the attack on my brother would never have happened. Spies aren't dishonest, untrustworthy people who make deals with teachers just to get rewards. They're people who care about other students and want to help them. I would be proud to be a spy!

2 Read the debate again. Complete the summaries of the two crimes. Write between one and three words in each gap.

Ellie
The crime: A ¹*girl* took ² ....
What happened next?
After she'd apologised, the criminal
³ .... school.

Finn
The crime: Some ⁴ ....
attacked and hurt ⁵ ....
What happened next?
The criminals got into trouble with
⁶ ....

3a Who uses these arguments? Write *F* for Finn, *E* for Ellie and *DK* for don't know.

1 Some spies will be dishonest.   *E*
2 Students can discover things teachers can't.   ....
3 Spies will stop most crimes.   ....
4 Spies can make some situations worse.   ....
5 Spies protect other students.   ....
6 Spies will only work for money.   ....

b Decide if the arguments are for (F) or against (A) school spies.

Listening

1 🔊 27 Listen to a radio interview. Who does Martin Fields work for?

M.........................

2 🔊 27 Listen again. According to Martin, are these facts true (T) or false (F)?

Spies:
1 need to be good at fighting.   *F*
2 must be very fit.   ....
3 must be very intelligent.   ....
4 spend lots of time following criminals.   ....
5 need good IT skills.   ....
6 usually work with others.   ....
7 have exciting lives.   ....
8 are quite unusual people.   ....

Writing An opinion essay

1 Read the heading quickly. Then put the parts of the essay (A–E) into the correct order.

'Celebrities have a right to privacy in their free time. It should be illegal for people to take photos without their permission.' What's your opinion?

A ....

Finally, another point to bear in mind is that photographers can be frightening. In 1997, Princess Diana's car crashed when she was trying to escape from photographers. If they hadn't chased her, perhaps she wouldn't have died.

B ....

In the first place, I feel that everyone has a right to privacy. There are times when all of us want to spend time alone, or just with friends or family.

C *1.*

Some people think that it should be illegal to take photos of celebrities without their permission. In my opinion, this new law would be an excellent idea.

D ....

In conclusion, my view is that taking photos of celebrities without their permission should be a crime. It isn't necessary and it can even be dangerous.

E ....

I also believe that spying on people is wrong. Some photographers take cover in celebrities' gardens, or they even break in to their homes. I think that this is very inappropriate behaviour.

2 Does the writer agree or disagree with the statement in the heading? What do you think?

....

3 Complete the phrases in the table.

Giving opinions
I ¹ *think* … In ² m..................... o.....................
Adding ideas and opinions
In the ³ f..................... p..................... , … I'm also convinced that … / I also believe that … Another point to ⁴ b..................... in m .... is … Finally, …
Concluding
To ⁵ c..................... , I believe that … In ⁶ c..................... , my v..................... is that …

4 Read the statement and question. In general, are you *for* or *against* this idea?

'It should be illegal for parents to spy on teenagers' phone or internet use without their permission.' What's your opinion?

5 Choose *three* ideas that support your opinion in Exercise 4. Then write your opinion essay. Use phrases from Exercise 3.

most teenagers are responsible
not all teenagers are honest
parents want to protect children
some teenagers may behave badly
teenagers have a right to privacy
trust is very important

....
....
....
....
....
....
....
....
....
....
....
....

9 Celebrate!

Vocabulary Party collocations

★ **1** Choose the correct option to make collocations.

1 wear *shallow / high / casual* clothes
2 wear *casual / high / party* heels
3 *do / make / throw* a party
4 do your *clothes / hair / decorations*
5 have *time / a time / the time* of your life
6 *greet / put / make* guests

★ **2** Complete the party invitations with the correct form of these verbs. Which party would you prefer?

do	make	travel	~~wear~~	wear

New Message ⊗

Hi all,

I'm really looking forward to the prom! Has everyone decided what smart clothes they're going to ¹*wear*? I know all the boys are going to ²........................ jackets and ties … it's harder for girls! ;)

Girls – meet at my house from 6.00 if you want to ³........................ your hair and make-up here.

Everyone else – meet here at 7.30 and we'll ⁴........................ to the prom by limo!!!!

We should get there just before the head girl and boy ⁵........................ their speeches.

Send

throw	~~wear~~	hire	put	stay

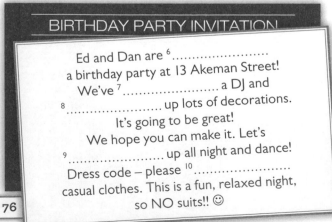

BIRTHDAY PARTY INVITATION

Ed and Dan are ⁶........................ a birthday party at 13 Akeman Street! We've ⁷........................ a DJ and ⁸........................ up lots of decorations. It's going to be great! We hope you can make it. Let's ⁹........................ up all night and dance! Dress code – please ¹⁰........................ casual clothes. This is a fun, relaxed night, so NO suits!! ☺

★★ **3** Last night Lois went to a party. Look at the pictures and write sentences about what happened. Use party collocations.

Last night …
1 Lois *did her hair*.   (hair)
2 She .... (dress/heels)
3 She .... (to the prom/limo)
4 She listened to Mr Brown, who .... (speech)
5 She danced and .... (time/life)
6 She .... and didn't go to bed until 6.30!   (all night)

Vocabulary page 112

Reading

1 Read the emails quickly. Answer the questions.

1 What happened yesterday? There was *a party*.
2 Where did it happen? At the ....
3 Who didn't go? ....
4 Why? He/She wasn't ....

2 Read the emails again. What things definitely happened at the party? (✓)

At the party, guests:

1 went for walks ✓
2 exchanged presents
3 wore jackets and ties
4 ate special food
5 danced
6 played a sport
7 stayed up all night
8 watched fireworks

3 Who generally liked or enjoyed these things? Complete the table, then answer the question below.

	Grace	Ryan
1 the decorations		☺
2 some guests' costumes		
3 the music		
4 the time of the party		
5 the food		
6 the beach game		

What did Grace and Ryan agree about?
They both ....

4 Complete the answers to the questions. Then answer the question below.

1 Why is the afternoon a good time for a party?
   It's *light enough to go for walks and play games*.
2 What did Blake wear?
   He .... and ....
3 What do we learn about Theo's brother?
   He helped to organise the party by

   ....
   Grace thinks he .... tell the truth!
4 How did Holly help with the party?
   She ....
5 Who cooked and what did he/she make?
   (Name *one* thing.)
   .... cooked. He/She ....

   ....

Do you think this sounds like a good party?
Why?/Why not?

....

New Message ✕

Send

Hi Sophie,

I said that I'd email you afterwards, so here goes!

I arrived around three. The afternoon is the perfect time to throw a party, because it was light enough for us to go for walks and play games. I know you'd told me that beach volleyball was fast, but I didn't realise *how* fast! The other players had fun, though – they must be fitter than me. ;)

Holly had made some (not very good!) decorations and Mal, Blake and Chris decided to look like idiots and wear surfer shirts and shorts, but apart from that, the 'Hawaiian' theme wasn't too embarrassing! I certainly can't complain about the food … mmm!

Theo's brother had hired a DJ, who set up speakers and lights on the beach. Theo said the DJ had worked in Ibiza, although you can't always believe everything Theo says! Everyone went wild to the music, though – including me. ;)

Get well soon!

Grace xxx

New Message ✕

Send

Hi Sophie,

Everyone told me to say 'hi' – we all missed you!

Holly had made flower and coconut decorations. She's such a good artist! Most people wore casual, everyday clothes, but Blake and his friends dressed like Hawaiian surfer dudes! Actually, they didn't look at all bad, but don't tell them that I said so. When it got dark, Jess's dad lit a fire and organised a barbecue. His Hawaiian pineapple kebabs were awesome!

I didn't really get into the music because rock's more my thing, but it was fun getting together with everyone at the beach, especially when we played volleyball! Everything finished too early, though. People want to stay up at a party!

I hope you're feeling better! Give me a call soon, OK?

Ryan

Grammar Reported statements

★ **1** Choose the correct options to report what people said about Ed's party. Then answer the question.

1 Marina said that she *is /(was)* having a great time *now /(then)*.

2 José *said / told* Zainab that *I / he* had been to better parties.

3 Rosie said that she *can't / couldn't* stand the other guests *here / there*.

4 Oscar told Zainab that he *is / was* going to dance all night *this night / that night*.

5 The twins *said / told* that *we / they* hadn't known about Ed's awful taste in music.

Which two guests are enjoying Ed's party the most? ....

★★ **2** Are the reported speech sentences correct (✓) or incorrect (✗)? Rewrite the incorrect sentences.

1 Tom: 'I'm having a party tomorrow.'
Tom said that he is having a party the next day. ✗
Tom said that he was having a party the next day.

2 me: 'I won't be home until late today.'
I said that I won't be home until late this day. ....
....

3 you → us: 'You must put the decorations up next week.'
You told us that you had to put the decorations up the following week. ....
....
....

4 we → they: 'The DJ won't play here.'
We said them that the DJ won't play there. ....
....

5 Ben: 'I've known Kate since we were young.'
Ben said that he'd known Kate since they were young. ....
....

Reported commands and requests

★★ **3** Complete the reported commands and requests. Who do you think might say these things at a party?

1 'Please turn the music down.'
They asked us *to turn* the music down.

2 'Take your shoes off!'
She told me .... my shoes off.

3 'Don't go in the bedrooms!'
They told guests .... in the bedrooms.

4 'Can you tidy up, please?'
He asked us ....

5 'Don't move the furniture.'
They told me .... the furniture.

6 'Please go home now!'
He asked us .... then.

Brain Trainer

When you rewrite a sentence, make sure that the second sentence has *exactly* the same meaning as the first sentence. Read *both* sentences carefully afterwards to check.

Now do Exercise 4.

★★ **4** Read the dialogue and decide whether the sentences are commands or requests. Rewrite the sentences in reported speech.

Mum [1] Hurry up! You're going to be late!

Josh I'm coming! Mum … [2] please can you give me a lift?

Mum Oh, OK, just this once! [3] Get in the car.

Josh Thanks! And [4] can you play some different music? I can't stand One Direction!

Mum No! [5] Don't change my music. If you don't like it – walk!

Josh OK, fine! But [6] please don't play it too loudly when we arrive. I don't want my friends to hear …

1 Josh's *mum told him to hurry up.*
2 Josh ....
3 Josh's mum ....
4 Josh ....
5 Josh's mum ....
6 Josh .... when they arrived.

Grammar Reference pages 102–103

Vocabulary Reporting verbs

Brain Trainer

Learn and use a variety of verbs to sound more interesting. For example, how many different alternatives to *say* and *tell* can you think of?

Now do Exercise 1.

★ 1 **Match the verbs (1–6) with the definitions (a–f).**

1 warn   *c*
2 refuse
3 promise
4 complain
5 explain
6 invite

a ask someone to an event
b say that you're annoyed about something
c tell someone about something bad that might happen
d say that you won't do something
e give information to help someone understand something
f say that you'll definitely do something

★ 2 **Which verb *can't* complete each sentence?**

1 I .... him not to be late.
  a told   b warned   ⓒ complained
2 She .... to help him to organise a party.
  a offered   b refused   c invited
3 They .... that they were going to the festival.
  a warned   b mentioned   c explained
4 We .... my gran to stay over Christmas.
  a invited   b asked   c offered
5 He .... that the party was very noisy.
  a warned   b complained   c admitted
6 My parents .... to pay for a limo!
  a agreed   b invited   c promised

★★ 3 **Complete the second sentence so that it has the same meaning as the first. Then answer the question.**

1 Matt: 'You're always breaking things, James!'
  Matt complained *that James was always breaking things.*
2 James: 'I'll pay for repairs.'
  James promised ....
3 Dora: 'I won't lend James any money this time!'
  Dora refused ....
4 Ben: 'I don't think it's an expensive table.'
  Ben mentioned ....
5 Katy: 'James was only dancing.'
  Katy explained ....
6 Emma: 'Everyone – my parents have just arrived!'
  Emma warned ....
What happened? ....

★★ 4 **Rewrite the underlined phrases in reported speech using these verbs.**

| admitted | complained | explained | ~~invited~~ |
| offered | promised | refused | |

A ¹ Would you like to come to my party this weekend, Brooke?
B Sounds great! ² I'll bring some music, if you like.
A Thanks, but that's OK. ³ My sister's organising the music.
B OK. ⁴ I'll bring some food! I'll make something special.
A Um … the thing is … I'm sorry, Brooke, but ⁵ I don't really like your cooking.
B Oh. Well, if that's how you feel, then ⁶ I'm not coming to your party.
A What? Don't be silly, Brooke. ⁷ You're being a bit selfish …

1 Aaron *invited Brooke to come to his party* that weekend.
2 Brooke .... ,
  if Aaron wanted her to.
3 Aaron ....
4 Brooke ....
5 Aaron ....
6 Brooke ....
7 Aaron ....

# Chatroom Reaching an agreement

Speaking and Listening

★ 1 🔊 28 **Choose the best options to complete the dialogue, then listen and check.**

W What do you fancy doing at the Notting Hill Carnival tomorrow, Eli?

E I think we ¹*could / should* watch the parades. That's what Notting Hill is famous for!

W That's a good ²*idea / thought*. ³*Maybe / Possibly* we can join in the dancing, too!

E ⁴*No / Not* way! You know I hate dancing, Willow. ⁵*How / Why* don't we have lunch afterwards, and eat some Caribbean food? We'll probably be hungry!

W That ⁶*does / makes* sense. OK, let's do that. Do you think we ⁷*could / may* get a bus there?

E No, I don't ⁸*agree / think* we should do that. Most of the roads will be closed! Let's walk. We can listen to the steel drum bands on the way!

★ 2 **Complete the conversations with these words.**

a good idea	Maybe we	sense	~~we could~~
we should (x2)	way	Why don't	

1 **A** Do you think *we could* travel by limo?
  B No ....! Limos are too expensive.

2 **A** I think .... all wear casual clothes.
  B That makes .... It's a party, not a prom!

3 **A** .... we walk?
  B I don't think .... walk there in the dark.

4 **A** .... can bring our own food.
  B That's .... It'll be cheaper.

★★ 3 🔊 29 **Gabriel and Carla are organising a surprise birthday party for their friend Yasmin. Listen and tick (✓) the problems you hear. Then answer the question.**

1 There isn't a DJ.
2 The guests are too busy to come.
3 There isn't any food.
4 There isn't a cake.
5 There aren't any decorations.
6 Someone hasn't been invited.

What is the biggest problem? Why?

....

★★ 4a 🔊 29 **Listen again. Who says these sentences, Gabriel (G) or Carla (C)?**

1 Do you think we could play the music ourselves? *G, S*
2 That makes sense. ....
3 Maybe we can buy one. ....
4 That's a good idea. ....
5 No way! ....
6 I don't think we should have black decorations. ....
7 Why don't we put up these? ....
8 I think you should phone her. ....

b Are the sentences making suggestions (*S*), agreeing (*A*) or disagreeing (*D*)?

★★ 5 **It's nearly the last day of term. Imagine that you and a friend want to do something special at the weekend to celebrate the start of the holidays. Write the conversation. Use the ideas below and expressions from Exercise 1 and 2.**

Your friend suggests an activity. (What?) You aren't interested. (Why?)
You suggest an activity. (What?) Your friend likes your idea.
Now agree when and where to meet.

Speaking and Listening page 121

Grammar Reported questions

★ **1a** **Choose the correct reported questions.**

1 'What time does the party start?'
   a She asked me what time the party started.
   b She asked me what time started the party.

2 'Did you have a good time?'
   a I asked him that he'd had a good time.
   b I asked him if he'd had a good time.

3 'Where can we put our coats?'
   a They asked me where could they put their coats.
   b They asked me where they could put their coats.

4 'How are you getting home?'
   a Elsie asked us how we were getting home.
   b Elsie asked us if we were getting home.

5 'Do I have to wear smart clothes?'
   a You asked her if you had to wear smart clothes.
   b You asked her if you did have to wear smart clothes.

6 'Will you need a taxi?'
   a Jamie asked me if I would a taxi need.
   b Jamie asked me if I would need a taxi.

b **Which of the questions were asked by:**

party guests?   ..1.....................
party organisers?   ....

★ **2** **Rewrite the reported questions in direct speech. Remember to change the words in bold as well as the word order.**

1 Tom asked her if **she was enjoying** the party.
   '*Are you enjoying* the party?' Tom asked her.

2 Mum asked what time everyone **was going** to arrive.
   'What time .... to arrive?' Mum asked.

3 They asked us if **they could help**.
   '.. ?' they asked us.

4 Robin asked me what time the limo **would arrive**.
   '.. ?' Robin asked me.

5 Kelly asked me if **I wanted** to dance.
   '.. to dance?' Kelly asked me.

6 I asked Nina how long **her** sister **had been** a DJ.
   '.. a DJ?' I asked Nina.

Grammar Reference pages 102– 103

★★ **3** **Write a reported question for each answer. Look at the words in bold to decide if you need to include a question word or expression.**

1 Belle asked *Aiden if he wanted any more cake*.
   'No, I don't want any more cake,' said Aiden.

2 Kayla asked ....
   '**Jackson** chose the music,' I told her.

3 Blake asked ....
   '**Yes,** we're going to come tonight,' we promised.

4 I asked ....
   'The bathroom is **on the left**,' Aimee explained.

5 Jack's sisters asked ....
   '**No,** I didn't enjoy the prom last night!' complained Jack.

6 We asked ....
   'I've been a DJ **for five years**,' Ella told us.

★★ **4** **Imagine you're a Hollywood celebrity! Rewrite the questions in reported speech. What would you reply?**

1 **'What skills do top actors have to have?'**
   Planet newspaper

2 **'Have you ever had any other jobs?'**
   Shh! website

3 'Will you star in any exciting new films soon?'
   Starz website

4 **'Which character are you going to play next?'**
   The Art Show

5 **'How did you become famous?'** *a fan*

6 **'Do you enjoy your fame?'** *Hiya magazine*

7 **'Where are you living?** *Celeb Living blog*

8 **'Can we come and stay with you?'**
   most of your family and friends

1 *Planet newspaper asked me what skills top actors had to have.*
2 ....
3 ....
4 ....
5 ....
6 ....
7 ....
8 ....

Reading

1 Read the What's On guide quickly. Which events might these festival visitors enjoy the most?

1 Alex loves sport.
2 Bryony is into comedy.
3 Josh wants to see a concert.
4 Fabio likes films.

WHAT'S ON AT THE EDINBURGH FESTIVAL

Scottish Galaxy readers' top recommendations

It's August. ¹ .d.. Last week we asked our readers to send in recommendations for the most 'must-see' events …

One Strange Lady

Clarissa Beddoes is performing her very funny and highly unusual show 'One Strange Lady' for the first time outside her homeland, the USA. ² …. Book tickets now if you want to find out why. There aren't many left! Readers who watched the show on her first night complained that their faces hurt afterwards because they'd laughed so much!

Scream Night

Stay up all night and watch all the best horror non-stop! The organisers promise to terrify you … in a good way! Readers have told us that last year's event was a lot of fun, with many fans wearing costumes to the cinema. Shows are rated 15+ from 11.00 to 21.00, and 18+ only after 21.00. ³ …. For example, your student card or a passport.

Roller Derby

Skating is a relaxing leisure activity, right? ⁴ …. Roller derbies are *fast*, and great fun to watch. The all-women teams wear colourful punk outfits and call themselves names like 'Killer Queen'. ⁵ …. As a result, crashes happen regularly. Readers have warned us not to sit too close to the front to avoid accidents!

Fireworks Finale

Many of you said that this was your favourite yearly event! Listen to the Scottish Chamber Orchestra play at the castle on the hill. ⁶ …. Even *more* magic is added by firework artists. ⁷ …. They're absolutely stunning. Don't worry if classical music isn't usually 'your thing'. Many readers have told us that this event made them think again!

2 Read the What's On guide again. Complete the gaps (1–7) with the missing sentences (a–g).

a Back there, she's already becoming a celebrity.
b For this reason, you'll need to bring I.D.
c In this beautiful setting, the music sounds magical.
d In Edinburgh, that means it's time for the biggest cultural festival in the world!
e What's more, they'll do *anything* to win!
f Not in these highly competitive events!
g You'll be amazed by their fire and light displays.

3 According to evidence in the guide, which event or events:

1 might encourage people to change their opinion of something?
Roller Derby, ...

2 may feature people who are dressed in unusual clothes?
.... , ...

3 won't be suitable for people of all ages?
....

4 might have a negative consequence for some visitors?
.... , ...

Listening

1 🔊 30 Listen to three friends discussing what to do at the Edinburgh festival. Number these events in the order you hear them? Which event do they decide to go to? (✓)

a a concert   ….
b a sports event ….
c a comedy show   ….
d a film night   .1.

2 🔊 30 Listen again and complete the table. Which event would *you* prefer?

Event	Cost	Reason for going/not going
1	£6	It sounds *boring*.
2	£..........	The performer isn't very ....
3	£..........	It's too ....
4	£..........	The tickets are .... and the food is ....

Writing A problem page

1 Read the problem and the reply. Complete the summary sentences.

Problem: Maya had a ¹*party*. Afterwards, her parents were ² .... !

Advice: You could offer to help pay for any damage. You could do ³ .... You should ⁴ ....

Problem page

Dear Dave,

My birthday party was a disaster! The night before, I'd mentioned the party online. ¹That was a mistake, because lots of extra guests arrived. Some of ²them made a mess in the house and they broke a few things! Mum and Dad were really angry. ³They told me I couldn't have any friends round until they could trust me again. That was a month ago! What should I do?

Maya

Dear Maya,

I'm very sorry to hear about your problem. I'm sure you feel bad about what happened, and that you won't make the same mistakes in the future! Social networking sites can be fun, but ⁴they aren't the right places to invite guests to a party – as you found out!

Have you offered to help pay for any damage? You could get a weekend job to earn some money. Why don't you try doing some extra housework at home, too? ⁵It might show your parents how responsible you are. Finally, ⁶my main piece of advice is to talk to your parents about the situation. Promise never to throw a party like that again, and ask them what you should do to win ⁷their trust back.

Good luck. ⁸Your parents won't stay angry forever, so be patient!

Dave

2 Look at the underlined pronouns and possessive adjectives (1–8) in the problem page. Match them to the meanings (a–h).

Pronouns
a Maya's parents
b mentioning the party online   *1*
c doing extra housework
d social networking sites
e the extra guests

Possessive adjectives
f relating to Maya
g relating to Dave
h relating to Maya's parents

3 Read the problem. Then read the advice below. What are your three favourite suggestions? You can choose your own ideas if you prefer.

Hello,

I really hope you can help! My best friend Sinead is going to a music festival next weekend, with her brother and sister, who are 19 and 20. Lots of my favourite bands are going to play there, but my parents have refused to let me go! They say I'm not old enough. What should I do? I really want to go!

Jackson, 16

- promise not to stay up all night
- explain how important the festival is to you
- promise to text or phone them from the festival
- introduce them to Sinead's brother and sister
- show them the festival website – especially the section about rules and safety!
- agree to do extra housework to prove that you're responsible
- promise to pay for the tickets yourself

4 Write a reply to the problem in Exercise 3. Use the paragraph plan below to help you. Include pronouns and possessive adjectives so that you don't repeat ideas.

Paragraph 1: Express sympathy with the writer.

Paragraph 2: Give advice, explaining your ideas. Include at least *three* pieces of advice.

Paragraph 3: End with some positive words and give some final advice.

Dear Jackson,

Check Your Progress 3

Grammar

1 Complete the sentences with the correct form of the verbs.

0 If we wait too long, it *will get* too dark to walk home. (get)

1 I asked him if he .... help me to write a speech. (can)

2 I .... to go into space if I had the chance. (love)

3 By the time the police tracked him down, he .... off his disguise. (already/take)

4 I .... to the party if I don't get an invitation! (not go)

5 They wouldn't have learnt the truth if they .... his phone. (not tap)

6 She asked her guests .... smart clothes. (wear)

/ 6 marks

2 Write the questions. Use *Who* or *What* and the correct Past simple form of the verb. Add an object (*you*) if necessary.

A [0] *Who took* this photo? (take)

B My mum, I think. It was such a special day.

A Why? [1] .... ? (happen)

B I passed my exams!

A Congratulations! [2] .... next? (do)

B I had a party, of course!

A [3] .... ? (invite)

B I invited my whole class.

A [4] .... ? (come)

B Everyone!

/ 4 marks

3 Rewrite the second sentence so that it has a similar meaning to the first.

0 'Don't follow me,' Tony told her.
Tony told her *not to follow him*.

1 'Why have you been so disloyal to me?' I asked her.
I asked her ....

2 The limo left. Then I arrived.
By the time I arrived, ...

3 'I'll hire a DJ tomorrow,' he said.
He said that ....

4 She decoded the message and caught the criminal.
If she hadn't ....

5 'Did you go to the party yesterday?' they asked me.
They asked me ....

/ 5 marks

Vocabulary

4 Choose the correct options.

British teen wins 'out of this world' prize

When Marcie Gray from the Space Agency called 18-year-old Dylan Hollings and told him that he'd won a trip into space, he thought she was [0] *C* lies! 'I'm afraid I was a little [1] ....polite to Marcie,' he says. 'I thought it was a joke!' Eventually, he realised that Marcie was telling the [2] .... , and that nothing she'd said had been [3] ....correct in any way. He really was going to take a seat inside a [4] .... and travel in an [5] .... around the earth!

The agency has [6] .... Dylan to attend a three-month space training course, and Marcie has [7] ....him that space travel isn't for everyone. The power of gravity isn't as [8] .... in space (it's much weaker), so it's more difficult to do [9] .... , everyday actions, like eating and walking. But Dylan is excited. 'I'm going to [10] ....the time of my life!' he says. He's already planning to [11] .... a huge party to celebrate when he returns. 'It would be [12] ....fair not to share the fun!' he says.

Dylan has [13] .... a deal with this newspaper, and he's agreed [14] .... his first interview to our reporters after he lands back on [15] ....Earth!

0 **a** saying   **b** speaking   **c** telling

1 **a** im   **b** un   **c** dis

2 **a** truth   **b** true   **c** honesty

3 **a** un   **b** im   **c** in

4 **a** telescope   **b** spacecraft   **c** asteroid

5 **a** galaxy   **b** comet   **c** orbit

6 **a** mentioned   **b** offered   **c** invited

7 **a** warned   **b** complained   **c** explained

8 **a** deep   **b** heavy   **c** strong

9 **a** strange   **b** ordinary   **c** shallow

10 **a** have   **b** make   **c** get

11 **a** greet   **b** throw   **c** put

12 **a** un   **b** im   **c** dis

13 **a** given   **b** put   **c** made

14 **a** us to give   **b** to give   **c** that he gives

15 **a** planet   **b** galaxy   **c** solar

/ 15 marks

Speaking

5 **Complete the conversation. Write one word in each gap.**

[Lily phones Oli]

Lily Oli, I need your advice! I've forgotten to buy Adam a birthday present. Should I tell him?

Oli No! I ⁰*wouldn't* tell him if I ¹......................... you, Oli. You know he'll be upset!

Lily Oh dear … The fact is ²......................... I've been really busy this week.

Oli Well, ³......................... don't you make him something?

Lily ⁴......................... way! I'm terrible at making things.

Oli Well, do you ⁵......................... you could make a chocolate cake? That isn't too difficult.

Lily That ⁶......................... sense. Thanks!

Oli I'll email you a good recipe. But make ⁷......................... you don't miss out any of the instructions! And ⁸......................... careful not to burn the cake!

[three hours later, Lily phones Oli again]

Lily Oli, help! I burnt the cake! You ⁹......................... to understand that I've never cooked before. I'm so sorry!

Oli OK, well, let's forget ¹⁰......................... it. I'm coming round. Maybe we can cook together.

Lily Thank you, you're amazing!

/ 10 marks

Translation

6 **Translate the sentences.**

1 After he'd escaped from prison, he broke into a house.

....

....

....

2 They asked the astronaut to make a speech.

....

....

....

3 Who stayed up all night to look at the stars?

....

....

....

4 I warned her not to wear high heels but she refused to listen.

....

....

....

5 They would have seen the comet if they hadn't been so impatient.

....

....

....

/ 5 marks

Dictation

7 🔊 31   **Listen and write.**

1 ....

....

2 ....

....

3 ....

....

4 ....

....

5 ....

/ 5 marks

Past simple vs Past continuous

Past simple
I played tennis. We didn't (did not) play tennis. Did you play tennis?   Yes, we did./No, we didn't.

Past continuous
I was playing tennis at two o'clock. We weren't (were not) playing tennis at two o clock. Were you playing tennis at two o'clock? Yes, we were./No, we weren't.

Past simple and Past continuous
When she arrived, he was playing tennis. While he was playing tennis, she arrived.

Irregular verbs have different Past simple forms. (See **Irregular verb list**, Workbook page 125).

Use

- We use the Past simple for actions that began and finished in the past.
  *I **did** my homework last night.*

- We use the Past continuous for actions that were in progress at a certain time in the past.
  *I **was doing** my homework at eight o'clock last night.*

Stative verbs

We rarely use stative verbs in the continuous form. The most common stative verbs are:

- verbs to express thoughts and opinions: *believe, know, understand, remember, forget, think (= believe).*

- verbs to express likes, preferences, needs or wants: *like, love, prefer, hate, need, want.*

- verbs to express state or possession: *be, have (got).*
  *We **think** it's a good idea.   I **love** cats.*

when and while

- We can use the Past simple and the Past continuous to describe an action that happened while another, longer action was in progress. We use the Past simple for the shorter action and the Past continuous for the longer action.

- To connect a Past simple and a Past continuous action, we often use *when* + Past simple or *while* + Past continuous.
  *We were talking **when** the teacher **arrived**.*
  *The teacher arrived **while** we **were talking**.*

- When we start a sentence with *when* or *while*, we use a comma.
  ***When** the teacher **arrived**, we were talking.*

used to

Affirmative		
I/He/She/It We/You/They	used to like	cartoons.

Negative		
I/He/She/It We/You/They	didn't (did not) use to like	school.

Questions and short answers
Did I/he/she/it/we/you/they use to like sweets? Yes, I/he/she/it/we/you/they did. No, I/he/she/it/we/you/they didn't.

Wh- questions
What games did you use to play when you were little?

Use

- We use *used to* for past habits or situations. We use *used to* to explain that the habit or situation no longer exists in the present.
  *I **used to read** comics (but now I don't).*
  *We **didn't use to** drink coffee (but now we do).*

- We can use *used to* OR the Past simple to talk about past habits or situations.
  *She **used to walk** to school every day.*
  *OR She **walked** to school every day.*

- We do not use *used to* to talk about single, completed past actions. We use the Past simple instead.
  *I **watched** TV last night.*
  NOT *I used to watch TV last night.*

Form

- In affirmative sentences, we use *used to* + infinitive.
  *We **used to swim** here.*

- In negative sentences and questions, we use *use to* (NOT *used to*) + infinitive. We use an auxiliary verb (*did/didn't*).
  *I **didn't use to eat** vegetables.*
  ***Did he use to live** here?*

Grammar practice

Past simple vs Past continuous

1 Choose the correct verb forms.

1 When the teacher (came)/ *was coming* in, everyone was talking.
2 This time last week I *lay / was lying* on the beach.
3 My mum met my dad while she *travel / was travelling* in the USA.
4 I'm sorry, I *didn't finish / wasn't finishing* my homework yesterday.
5 He *broke / was breaking* his leg while he was playing football.
6 We *didn't look / weren't looking* at the camera when she took the photo.

2 Complete the conversation with the Past simple or Past continuous form of the verbs.

Mum ¹ *Did you do* (you/do) lots of studying at the library this afternoon, Jas?

Jas Er, yes, thanks. I ² .... (study) really hard all afternoon!

Mum Really? What ³ .... (you/do) at four p.m.? I ⁴ .... (not see) you in the library, so you ⁵ .... (not study) right then.

Jas Oh, er … Erin saw me while she ⁶ .... (walk) past. We ⁷ .... (have) a break for coffee. But while we ⁸ .... (sit) in the café, we tested each other on English questions. Ask Erin if you don't believe me!

3 Write sentences or questions. Use the Past simple or Past continuous form of the verbs.

1 Last year / I / win / a scholarship
Last year I won a scholarship.
2 At eight o'clock last night / we / play / computer games
....
3 They / not live / here / three years ago
....
4 I / not sleep / when / you / phone
....
5 She / not work / when / I / see / her
....
6 You / ask him his name / while / you / dance / ?
....

used to

4 Write sentences with *used to* and *didn't use to* to talk about what life was like 1,000 years ago.

1 people / drive cars
People didn't use to drive cars.
2 many British children / work
....
3 people / live as long
....
4 cities / be smaller
....
5 teenagers / wear jeans
....
6 some people / think / the Earth was flat
....

5 Complete the sentences and questions with the correct form of *used to* and the verb.

1 We *didn't use to see* (not see) each other very often.
2 **A** Where .... (you/go) on holiday?
  B We .... (visit) my grandparents in Madrid.
3 I .... (not like) going swimming.
4 **A** .... (they/play) basketball with you?
  B No, they ....
5 **A** .... (she/sit) next to you in class?
  B Yes, she ....

6 Rewrite the sentences and questions with the correct form of *used to*.

1 I loved playing card games.
I used to love playing card games.
2 We were good friends.
....
3 My sister didn't drink much coffee.
....
4 How often did he call you?
....
5 Our neighbours had a noisy dog.
....
6 **A** Did your dad work here?
  B No, he didn't.
....?
....

Grammar Reference 2

Present perfect

Present perfect + ever, never, already, yet

The village's success on the football pitch has been huge.

Have you ever played football?

We watch football on TV but we have never played it.

You've already formed a football team, but you haven't found a pitch yet!

Present perfect + just

Just means very recently.
I've just finished my homework!

Irregular verbs have different past participle forms. (See **Irregular verb list**, Workbook page 125).

Use

We use the Present perfect to talk about:

- states, actions or events that started in the past and continue in the present.
  *How long **have** you **known** her?*

- past experiences, without saying exactly when they happened.
  I've been to many different countries.

- past events or situations which have a result in the present.
  I've lost my notebook, so I can't do my homework!

ever and never

- We use ever and never (= not ever) to refer to 'any time up to now'.
- We use ever/never before the past participle.
  *Have you **ever** been abroad?*
  *I've **never** written a novel.*

already, just and yet

- We use already in affirmative sentences to emphasise that an action has happened.
  *You've **already** made a difference to people's lives.*

- We use just in affirmative sentences to emphasise that an action has happened very recently.
  *She's **just** left. She left a few seconds ago!*

- We use already and yet before the past participle.

- We use yet in negative sentences to talk about an action that has not been completed, but which the speaker hopes will be completed in the future.
  *I haven't seen the photo **yet**. I'd like to see it soon!*

- We use yet in questions to ask if an action has been completed.
  *Have you finished your homework **yet**?*

- We use yet at the end of negative sentences and questions.

Present perfect with since and for

Since 2008, John has visited six countries.
I have now worked at the supermarket for two years.

Use

- We use for and since to answer the question *How long … ?*
  ***How long** have you been here? I've been here **for five days**./**since Sunday**.*

- We use for to refer to a period of time.
  For example: **for** hours/two days/a month/a year/ my whole life/ages/a while/ever.
  *I've worked here **for two weeks**.*
  *He's been away **for a long time**.*

- We use since to talk about a point in time.
  For example: **since** lunch/yesterday/last week/May/ 2010/my birthday/I was young.
  *I've lived here **since April**.*
  *She's kept in touch **since she moved to France**.*

Present perfect vs Past simple

Present perfect

Nancy has written two novels.

Past simple

They practised for hours every day.

Use

- We use the Present perfect to talk about a state or action that happened in the past that has a result in the present, or which continues in the present.

- We also use the Present perfect when we want to talk about a past event without saying exactly when it happened.
  He's already left. (It doesn't matter when he went.)
  I've lived here for two years. (I still live here now.)

- We use the Past simple to talk about a state or action that finished in the past. We also use the Past simple to say exactly when something happened. We often use a time expression (*yesterday, last night*, etc.).
  *I lived here **in 1992**.   He left **last night**.*

Grammar practice

Present perfect + *ever, never, already, just, yet, since* and *for*

1 Write questions with the Present perfect and *ever*. Answer them with the Present perfect and *never*.

1 you / jump out / of a plane / ?
Have you ever jumped out of a plane?
No, I've never jumped out of a plane.

2 you / meet / the President of the USA / ?
....
No, ...

3 your dad / win / a skateboarding contest / ?
....
No, ...

2 Write Present perfect sentences. Include the word in brackets.

1 my brother / arrive   (just)
My brother's just arrived.

2 you / speak / to her / ?   (yet)
....

3 we / leave / school   (just)
....

4 I / eat / lunch   (already)
....

5 Ben / not hear / the song   (yet)
....

6 they / pay / you / ?   (yet)
....

3 Complete the text. Use the Present perfect form of the verbs with *for* or *since*.

I ¹ *'ve lived in this city since* (live/in this city) I was born. I ² .... (live/ in this house) the last twelve years. My gran ³ .... (live/in this house) her whole life. I ⁴ .... (have/my own room) I was eight. It ⁵ .... (change/a lot) then. It used to have pink walls – yuck! The walls ⁶ .... (be/green) a long time – and they're now covered in posters.

4 Complete the conversation with these time expressions.

already	ever	for	just
never	since	~~yet~~	yet

Faith Have you finished packing for the holiday ¹*yet*?

Jack I've ² .... started! I began about five minutes ago. I haven't got very far ³ .... I never know what to take.

Faith Well, I've ⁴ .... packed my bag. I did it last night. So I could help you now, if you liked. I'm so excited! I've ⁵ .... been to the USA before. Have you ⁶ .... been there?

Jack A few times, but I haven't been ⁷ .... years. In fact, I haven't been there ⁸ .... I was ten.

Present perfect vs Past simple

5 Choose the best options.

1 A How many times ⟨have you been⟩ / did you go to Australia?
  B I *'ve never been / never went* to Australia.
2 I *'ve bought / bought* this bike last year.
3 *Have you told / Did you tell* her yet?
4 When I *'ve been / was* eight I *'ve started / started* learning the piano.
5 We *haven't seen / didn't see* you for ages. How *have you been / were you*?
6 The city *has changed / changed* a lot since we first *have moved / moved* here.

6 Complete the sentences. Use the Present perfect or the Past simple form of the verbs.

1 *Did you hear* (you/hear) the storm last night?
2 This is the first time I .... (see) this film.
3 She .... (travel) abroad many times since she became famous.
4 Shakespeare .... (write) poems as well as plays.
5 Wow! I .... (never/see) a shark before.
6 They .... (make) it to the finals last week.
7 I feel sorry for him. He .... (have) bad luck all his life.

Grammar Reference ③

Gerunds and infinitives

Use

Use the gerund (*-ing* form):	
after certain verbs	Please stop shouting!
after prepositions	I'm interested in studying emotions.
as the subject or object of a sentence	Smiling makes you happier.

Use the infinitive (with *to*):	
after certain verbs	I tried to smile.
after certain adjectives	It's wrong to lie.
to explain the purpose of an action	I phoned them to complain.

Form

We form the negative by putting *not* before the gerund or the infinitive.
*Imagine **not smiling** for a month!*
*I decided **not to go**.*

Verb + gerund

- These are some of the verbs which commonly take the gerund:

  advise   can't stand   consider   discuss
  dislike   enjoy   finish   hate   imagine
  keep   like   love   mention   (don't) mind
  miss   practise   prefer   recommend
  regret   stop   suggest

  *I **hate blushing**.*
  *He **can't stand screaming**.*

Verb + infinitive

- These are some of the verbs which commonly take the infinitive:

  afford   agree   appear   arrange   ask
  choose   decide   expect   hope   learn
  manage   mean   need   offer   plan
  pretend   promise   remember   refuse
  seem   try   wait   want

  *They **agreed to help**.*
  *I **decided to stay**.*

Adjective + infinitive

- These are some of the adjectives which commonly take the infinitive:

  difficult   easy   embarrassed   happy
  important   lucky   ready   right   sad
  stupid   surprised   wrong

  *I was **surprised to see** her.*
  *You were **lucky to survive**.*

Present perfect continuous

Affirmative		
He/She/It	's (has) been waiting	for ages
I/You/We/They	've (have) been waiting	

Negative		
He/She/It	hasn't (has not) been waiting	for long
I/You/We/They	haven't (have not) been waiting	

Questions and short answers
Has he/she/it been waiting long?
Yes, he/she/it has.
No, he/she/it hasn't.
Have I/you/we/they been waiting long?
Yes, I/you/we/they have.
No, I/you/we/they haven't.

Wh- questions
How long have you been waiting?

Use

We use the Present perfect continuous:

- to emphasise the length of a longer action which started in the past and continues until the present.
  *I'm tired. I**'ve been working** hard all day.*
  *Where have you been? Jo**'s been looking** for you for hours!*

- to talk about an action that finished recently and which has a result in the present.
  *I'm sweating because I**'ve been running**.*
  *She's wet because she**'s been swimming**.*

We can use *for* and *since* with the Present perfect continuous.
*It's been raining **for days**.*
*We've been studying **since lunch**.*

Grammar practice

Gerunds and infinitives

1 Complete the sentences with the gerund or infinitive form of the verb *swim.*

1 It's good *to swim*.
2 I prefer ....
3 .... is my favourite sport.
4 I went to the pool ....
5 I tried ....
6 I'm not keen on ....

2 Write the gerund or infinitive form of the verbs.

1 We hope you enjoy *visiting* (visit) the sports hall.
2 If you're interested in .... (find) out about classes, please ask.
3 Please remember .... (follow) the rules.
4 .... (smoke) isn't allowed in the hall.
5 Please try .... (not/leave) anything behind.
6 Always buy a ticket! .... (not/pay) to use the facilities is theft.

3 Complete the text with the gerund or infinitive form of these verbs.

attend	be	become	invent
make	perform	tell	

¹*Being* a professional comedian is a difficult job! It isn't easy ² .... original ideas, and ³ .... in front of audiences can be scary. You have to work long hours if you want ⁴ .... successful, and you have to travel a lot ⁵ .... performances. But if you like ⁶ .... jokes and you're good at ⁷ .... people laugh, it might be the job for you.

Present perfect continuous

4 Are these sentences correct (✓) or incorrect (✗)?

1 He's been smiling all day. ✓
2 I've been studied English since I was little.
3 My dog hasn't been eating well recently.
4 How long have they been living here?
5 Have you been working here long? No, I don't.
6 We've been knowing her for years.

5 Complete the conversation with the Present perfect continuous form of the verbs.

Tom You look tired.
Bella Yes, we ¹ *'ve been working* (work) hard since lunch!
Cate I ² .... (garden) in the rain! It ³ .... (rain) all day.
Bella I ⁴ .... (not help) in the garden, but I ⁵ .... (cook) in the kitchen for hours.
Cate What ⁶ .... (you/do) all day, Tom? ⁷ .... (you/work)?
Tom No, I ⁸ .... I ⁹ .... (relax)!

6 Write sentences and questions. Use the Present perfect continuous form of the verbs in bold and add *for* or *since*.

1 the children / **play** / three hours
The children have been playing for three hours.
2 She / **cry** / she / read his text
....
3 We / **drive** / 8.30 this morning
....
4 you / **wait** / hours / ?
....
5 I / **not study** / Mandarin / very long
....
6 They / **not speak** / to each other / the argument
....
....

Modal verbs: general points

Use

We use modal verbs before other verbs to add a special meaning to a sentence (for example, ability, advice, etc.).

Form

- We put an infinitive without *to* after most modal verbs:
  We **must go**.   I **can hear** them.
- We do not add an *-s* to modal verbs in the third person (with *he*, *she* or *it*).
  He **can** stay.   It **should** stop.
- We do not use *do/does* with modal verbs to form negatives, questions or short answers.
  He **might not** come.
  Can I see her? No, you **can't**.
- *Have to* is not a modal verb. We use *have to* differently:
  She **has to hurry**.   I **don't have to leave**.
  Do I have to wait? Yes, you **do**.

Modals: ability, obligation, prohibition, advice

Ability
We can reduce the number of people who die.
We can't stop natural disasters.

Obligation
You must come to the school now.
They have to live on flat land near the sea.
We don't have to lose huge numbers of lives.

Prohibition
You mustn't leave the shelter.

Prohibition
You should listen to the warnings.
You shouldn't go near the sea.

Ability: *can, can't (cannot)*

- We use *can* or *can't* to talk about ability in the present.
  He **can play** the guitar.
  I **can't see** you in the dark.
  NOT I **don't see** you in the dark.

Obligation: *must, have to, don't have to*

- We use *must* or *have to* (which is not a modal verb) to talk about obligation in the present.
  You **must do/have to do** your homework.
- We use *don't have to* when there is NO obligation. We cannot use *mustn't* in this way.
  You **don't have to** come. It's your choice.
  NOT You **mustn't come**. It's your choice.

Prohibition: *mustn't (must not)*

- We use *mustn't* to express a strong prohibition.
  You **mustn't talk** here – it isn't allowed!
  NOT You **don't have to talk** here – it isn't allowed!

Advice: *should, shouldn't (should not)*

- We use *should* to ask for and give advice or make recommendations.
  What **should** I **do**? You **should call** for help.
- We use *shouldn't* to say that we think something is a bad idea.
  You **shouldn't swim** in that river – it's very deep.

Past modals

People could use schools as shelters.
I couldn't speak English when I was six.
They had to teach children about the dangers.
They didn't have to wait long for the next cyclone.

We use different verb forms to talk about the past.

Ability in the past: *could, couldn't (could not)*

- We use *could* or *couldn't* to talk about ability in the past. We don't use *can* or *can't*.
  She **could ski** when she was six.
  NOT She **can ski** when she was six.
  I **couldn't read** when I was two.
  NOT I **can't read** when I was two.

Obligation in the past: *had to, didn't have to*

- We use *had to* or *didn't have to* to talk about obligation in the past.
  She **had to wear** a uniform at primary school.
  We **didn't have to go** to school last Monday.
- We cannot use *must* for obligation in the past. We use *had to* instead.
  She **must had to** wear a uniform at primary school.

Modals: possibility

That bite must hurt.
It might be a poisonous snake.
The bite could be really dangerous.
The snake can't be deadly.

Possibility: *could, might, might not*

- We use *could*, *might* and *might not* to suggest present or future possibility.
  *You **could be** right – I'm not sure.*
  *The weather **might be** cold tomorrow. I don't know.*
  *He **might not come**. He hasn't decided yet.*

Impossibility and certainty: *can't (cannot), must*

- We use *can't* when we think or guess that something is impossible.
  *He **can't be** in Africa. I saw him in town this morning!*
  *Being an explorer **can't be** easy.*

- We use *must* when we think or guess that something is certain.
  *That man **must feel** scared. That snake looks terrifying!*
  *It **must be** late. It's getting dark.*

Grammar practice

Modals: ability, obligation, prohibition, advice

1 **Complete the text with these words.**

~~can~~	can't	don't have to
must	mustn't	should

Anyone ¹*can* learn surfing – but it takes a little time. You ² .... learn with a teacher – many people don't. However, if you want my advice you ³ .... take at least one class. It's a really good idea!

Of course, you ⁴ .... be able to swim first. This is essential. If you ⁵ .... swim, you absolutely ⁶ .... try surfing – don't even think about it!

2 **Rewrite the second sentence so that it has a similar meaning to the first.**

1 I don't know how to ski.   (can)
  I *can't ski*.
2 It's a good idea to exercise.   (should)
  You ....
3 Don't swim here!   (must)
  You ....
4 Wearing safety glasses is optional.   (have to)
  You ....
5 He knows how to skate.   (can)
  He ....

Past modals

3 **Put the modals into the past form.**

1 She *could* (can) play the violin when she was six.
2 We .... (have to) work hard last year.
3 I .... (can) speak German when I was five.
4 You .... (don't have to) help her yesterday.
5 He .... (can't) do last night's homework.

Modals: possibility

4 **Choose the best option.**

1 It *might* / *must* / *can't* be sunny tomorrow. I hope so!
2 It *could* / *must* / *can't* be her birthday. She had a birthday party last month!
3 You *can't* / *could* / *must* be right I'm not sure.
4 Being in a tornado *must* / *can't* / *could* be terrifying, that's for certain.
5 I *must* / *can't* / *might* have some water in my bag. Hang on – I'll look.

5 **Complete the sentences. Write *could*, *might*, *can't* or *must*.**

1 He *could* be her brother. I don't know what her brother looks like!
2 She .... be good at Maths. She got top marks in her exam!
3 You .... be tired. We've only been walking for ten minutes!
4 She .... be at home. I'm not sure where she is.
5 They .... be cold. They're shivering!

will/going to

will
He'll (will) help you.
I won't (will not) help you.
Will you help me?
Yes, we will./No, we won't.

going to
She's (is) going to work here.
We aren't (are not) going to work here.
Are you going to work here?
Yes, I am./No, I'm not.

Future time expressions

Tonight/Tomorrow, …
Next week/month/year …
This summer/weekend …
In a day/three days' time …
By Monday/the weekend/the end of the year …
In the next week/month/year …

Use

We use *will*:

- to express sudden decisions or thoughts made at the moment of speaking. These include offers, promises, requests, or orders.
  A *I'm cold.*   **B** *I'll close the window.*
  ***Will** you **get** here at nine tomorrow, please?*

- to make or ask for a general prediction or guess about the future.
  *Who do you think **will get** the job?*
  *I think he'**ll be** famous one day.*

We use *going to*:

- to talk about general plans or intentions for the future.
  *I'**m going to study art** at university.*
  *He'**s going to speak** to the manager tomorrow.*

- to make predictions based on evidence at the moment of speaking.
  *Look at those clouds. It'**s going to rain**.*
  *Watch out! We'**re going to crash**!*

Present simple and Present continuous for future

Present simple for future
The train leaves at 11.43 tomorrow.
The next bus doesn't (does not) leave until lunchtime.
Does the concert start at eight?
Yes, it does./No, it doesn't.

Present continuous for future
I'm (am) starting my new job next week.
We aren't (are not) meeting them tonight.
Are you doing anything interesting this summer?
Yes, we are./No, we aren't.

Use

- We use the Present simple to talk about scheduled events or timetables.
  *The next train **arrives** in ten minutes.*
  *The shops **shut** at half past five.*

- We use the Present continuous to talk about definite plans. We often mention a time or place.
  *We'**re celebrating** Sara's birthday **this weekend**.*
  *I'**m meeting** them **outside the cinema at eight o'clock**.*

- We do not use the Present simple to talk about plans.
  *Ella **is meeting** us here tonight.*
  *NOT Ella **meets** us here tonight.*

Grammar practice

will/going to

1 Match the uses (a–d) to the verbs in bold in sentences (1–6).

a plan or intention
b spontaneous decision
c general prediction
d prediction based on evidence

1 I think you**'ll be** a very successful journalist.   *c*
2 We**'re going to study** German next year.
3 A These books are heavy.
    B I**'ll carry** them.
4 It's snowing. It**'s going to feel** cold today.
5 I probably **won't have** the same job all my life.
6 I**'m not going to eat** lunch in the office today.

2 Complete the future time expressions.

by (x2)   in (x2)   ~~next~~   next

1 He's going to start a new job *next* week.
2 I'll call you .... two days' time.
3 We'll know the answer .... Sunday.
4 I'll finish the project some time ....
the next week.
5 We're going to move house ....
month.
6 I'm going to write the report ....
the end of the day.

3 Choose the correct options.

1 A I've lost my presentation!
    B Don't worry, I *'ll* / I'm going to help you.
2 He's coming this way! He *'ll* / *'s going to* walk right past us!
3 Have you decided what to do next? *Will you* / *Are you going to* text her?
4 A I'm really tired.
    B I *'ll* / *'m going to* get you a coffee.
5 A Have you got any plans for tonight?
    B Yes, I *'ll* / *'m going to* meet some friends.
6 I *won't* / *'m not going to* want to work here in twenty years' time.

4 Complete the sentences with *will* or *going to* and the verbs.

1 She*'s going to leave* (leave) school next year.
2 Life .... (not stay) the same forever!
3 Be careful! You .... (drop) those cups!
4 A The phone's ringing.
    B I .... (answer) it.
5 We .... (not spend) this summer at home.
6 What .... (the world/be) like in 2050?

Present simple and Present continuous for future

5 Choose the correct options.

Allie [1] *Do you get /* Are you getting *a train into town tonight?*

Ian Yes. Mum [2] *gives / is giving* me a lift to the station after dinner. The train [3] *leaves / is leaving* at 7.25.

Allie What time [4] *does it arrive / is it arriving*?

Ian At 7.50.

Allie But we [5] *meet / 're meeting* everyone at 8.00!

Ian I know, don't panic! The film [6] *starts / is starting* at 8.15. There's plenty of time.

6 Write sentences with the Present simple or the Present continuous.

1 The office / open / at 8.30
The office opens at 8.30.
2 Her plane / land / at midnight tonight
....
3 I / give / a presentation / here tomorrow
....
4 he / work / late / tonight / ?
....
5 The next bus / not stop / on Main Street
....
6 We / not use the meeting room / after lunch
....

Passive statements

	Active	*Passive*
Present simple	They repair the pier.	The pier is repaired.
Past simple	They repaired the pier.	The pier was repaired.
Future simple	They will repair the pier.	The pier will be repaired.

Use

We use the passive when we are more interested in talking about an action (the verb) than saying who or what does/did it (the agent).

The sea wall **will be rebuilt** *next week.*
(Information about who will build the seawall is unknown or not important.)

The sandcastle **was washed** *away by the sea.*
(We are particularly interested in the sandcastle and what happened to it.)

Form

- To form the passive, we use *(not)* be + past participle. We use *be* in the same tense that we would use in the active sentence.
  They **make** *the ice cream here.* (Present simple active) → *The ice cream* **is made** *here.* (Present simple passive)

- When we change an active sentence into a passive sentence, the object of the active sentence becomes the subject of the passive sentence. We put this noun at the start of the passive sentence.

        (object)
      ‾‾‾‾‾‾‾‾‾‾
They **restored** *the deckchair.*

The deckchair **was restored**.
  (subject)

by + agent

- If we want to include information about who or what does/did the action in a passive sentence, we use *by* + agent.

  (subject)   (object)
 ‾‾‾‾‾‾‾‾‾‾   ‾‾‾‾‾‾‾‾‾‾
Eugenius Birch **designed** *Brighton's West Pier.*

Brighton's West Pier **was designed by** *Eugenius Birch.*
  (subject)   (agent)

- We include *by* + agent if the agent is important:
  Brighton's West Pier was designed. ✗
  (This sentence is incomplete!)
  Brighton's West Pier was designed **by Eugenius Birch**. ✓ (This is a complete sentence. The information about Eugenius Birch is important.)

- We omit *by* + agent if we do not know who or what the agent is, or if the agent is not important.
  My bag was stolen.
  NOT ~~My bag was stolen **by someone**~~.
  (I don't know who stole my bag.)

  The bridge will be painted.
  NOT ~~The bridge will be painted **by some painters**~~.
  (It isn't important to say who will paint the bridge.)

Passive questions

	Active	*Passive*
Present simple	Do they make it here?	Is it made here? Yes, it is./No, it isn't.
Past simple	Did they make it here?	Was it made here? Yes, it was./No, it wasn't.
Future simple	Will they make it here?	Will it be made here? Yes, it will./No, it won't.

Wh- **questions**		

Active	**Passive**
Where do they sell them?	Where are they sold?
When did they build it?	When was it built?
What will they discover?	What will be discovered?

Form

- To form passive questions, we use the correct form of *be* + past participle.
  Was it restored *here?*

- If we need to include a subject in present and past passive questions, we put it after the verb *be:*
  Where **is the ice cream** *made?*

- If we need to include a subject in future simple passive questions, we put it after *will* and before *be:*
  Where **will the seagulls be** *released?*

- If we need to include *by* + agent, we add it to the end of the question:
  Was the photo taken **by your grandmother**?

- If we want to ask who or what an agent is/was, we use *by* at the end of the question:
  Who was the photo taken **by**?

Grammar practice

Passive statements

1 Write the tense: *present*, *past*, or *future*. Then decide if the sentence is *active* or *passive*.

1 They **discovered** an island.
   past   active
2 English **is spoken** here.
   ....
3 We**'ll visit** the coast.
   ....
4 The pier **wasn't repaired**.
   ....
5 The hut **will be painted** soon.
   ....
6 Sorry, we **don't accept** Euros.
   ....

2 Write the correct present, past or future passive form of the verbs.

1 The new arcade *will be opened* (open) next year.
2 The church .... (build) in the sixteenth century.
3 The café .... (clean) every night.
4 The beach .... (not/discover) until 1540.
5 The wild birds .... (not/release) tomorrow.
6 Sharks .... (not/see) here very often these days.

3 Rewrite the sentences in the passive. Begin the passive sentence with the noun in bold. Only include *by* + agent where shown.

1 Homer wrote **The Odyssey**.
   The Odyssey was written by *Homer.*
2 People will film **the documentary** here.
   ....
3 Animal experts train **the dolphins**.
   .... by ....
4 They organise **the event** every year.
   ....
5 Someone took **the photo** last year.
   ....
6 Wild animals won't eat **the food**.
   .... by ....

4 Cross out *by* + agent when it isn't necessary.

1 The fish are caught locally ~~by people~~.
2 The town will be visited **by the Queen**.
3 My bag was stolen **by someone** yesterday.
4 This coast was painted **by Van Gogh**.
5 The house will be built **by builders** next year.
6 All the souvenirs are made **by local people**.

Passive questions

5 Make passive questions.

1 made / the / sandcastles / How / are / ?
   How are the sandcastles made?
2 born / were / you / Where / ?
   ....
3 held / Is / surfing contest / the / here / ?
   ....
4 treasure / Will / the / ever / discovered / be / ?
   ....
5 prizes / awarded / will / How / be / many / ?
   ....
6 the / earthquake / destroyed / Were / the / buildings / in / ?
   ....
   ....

6 Write passive questions. Use the tenses given.

1 you / bite / ?   (past)
   Were you bitten?
2 it / break / ?   (present)
   ....
3 When / it / invent / ?   (past)
   ....
4 the ship / save / ?   (future)
   ....
5 Where / the deckchairs / keep / ?   (present)
   ....
6 How long / the beach / close / ?   (future)
   ....

First and Second conditional

First conditional

I'll (will) call you if I have time.
If they don't (do not) take a map, they won't (will not) find the island.
What will you do if it's (is) sunny tomorrow?

Second conditional

If I discovered a new star, I'd (would) be very happy.
He wouldn't travel into space if he didn't work for NASA.
If you had your own spacecraft, where would you go?

- Conditional sentences have two clauses: the conditional clause (starting with *if*) and the result clause.
  If I had lots of money, I'd travel round the word.
  (conditional clause)   (result clause)
- We can use the clauses in any order, but we must use a comma when the conditional clause comes first.
  If I were you, I'd go. = I'd go if I were you.

First conditional

- We use the First conditional to talk about possible or probable future events or situations.
  I'll talk to her if she goes to the party.
  (She might go to the party. It's quite likely.)
- We also use the First conditional to make promises and give warnings.
  I'll help you if you buy me a coffee.
  If you don't take a map, you'll get lost!
- To form the First conditional, we use:
  if + Present simple, *will/won't* + infinitive
  If you **work** harder, you**'ll improve**.
  OR
  will/won't + infinitive + *if* + Present simple
  *You**'ll improve if** you **work** harder.*

Second conditional

- We use the Second conditional to talk about unlikely or impossible present or future events or situations.
  I'd buy a spacecraft if I became a billionaire.
  (I probably won't become a billionaire. It isn't very likely.)
- We also use the Second conditional to give advice:
  I wouldn't do that if I were you.

- To form the Second conditional, we use:
  if + Past simple, *would(n't)* + infinitive
  If he **discovered** a new island, he**'d be** very happy.
  OR
  would(n't) + infinitive + *if* + Past simple
  *He**'d be** very happy **if** he **discovered** a new island.*

Subject/Object questions

Subject questions

Which costs more?
Who discovered the island?

Object questions

How much does it cost?
What did he discover?

- When the question word is the object of a Present simple or Past simple question, we use *do/does/did*.
  How do **you** feel?
  (object) (subject)

  Who did **he** see?
  (object) (subject)
- When the question word is the subject of a Present simple or Past simple question, we do NOT use *do/does/did*.
  What happens now?
  (subject)

  Who saw **you**?
  (subject)   (object)

Grammar practice

First and Second conditional

1 Match the sentences beginnings (1–6) with the endings (a–f) to make sentences. Do the completed sentences include First (*1st*) or Second (*2nd*) conditional forms?

1 If I were an astronaut, _f._ (_2nd_)
2 If you look into the telescope, ... (.......)
3 If we see a comet tonight, ... (.......)
4 If the river wasn't so wide, ... (.......)
5 If I didn't love adventure, ... (.......)
6 If it's cloudy at night, ... (.......)

a I'll be surprised.
b the stars won't shine as brightly.
c you'll see the planet Venus.
d we'd be able to cross it.
e I wouldn't be an explorer.
f I'd travel to Mars.

2 Choose the correct options.

1 If you wait here, I *'ll* / *'d* get the tickets.
2 If we had a map, we *'d* / *'ll* know where to go next.
3 I'll go with you if you *like* / *liked*.
4 I *won't* / *wouldn't* be happy if they cancel the trip.
5 If I met an alien, I *won't* / *wouldn't* know what to say!
6 Where would you go if you *had* / *have* your own spacecraft?

3 Decide if the situations (1–6) are likely or unlikely for these speakers. Then complete the gaps with the correct form of the verbs to make First or Second conditional sentences.

1 Your mum: If I *were* (be) rich, I*'d travel* (travel) the world.
2 Famous singer: If I .... (travel) the world, I .... (meet) lots of fans.
3 Astronaut: I .... (keep) a video diary if I .... (go) into space.
4 You: If I .... (go) into space, I .... (look) for aliens!
5 Your neighbour: I .... (not know) what to do if I .... (see) a tiger here!
6 Nature film-maker: If we .... (not see) a tiger, we .... (be) disappointed.

Subject/Object questions

4 Are these questions subject questions (*S*) or object questions (*O*)?

1 Who helps you? *S*
2 Who do you help? ....
3 What moved? ....
4 What did they move? ....
5 How much does it weigh? ....
6 Which weighs more? ....

5 Write subject and object questions. Add an auxiliary verb (*do/does/did*) if necessary.

1 What kind of holiday / you / usually / ? (prefer)
What kind of holiday do you usually prefer?
2 What / last weekend / ? (happen)
....
3 Who / he / yesterday / ? (see)
....
4 Who / her / to dinner / last night / ? (invite)
....
5 How fast / this spacecraft / ? (fly)
....
6 How many / people / in your house / ? (live)
....

6 Write subject and object questions for the underlined information in the answers.

1 *Which one looks better*? (look)
The red one looks better.
2 ....? (text)
I texted John.
3 ....? (eat)
We ate fish and chips.
4 ....? (give)
Mum gives me the money.
5 ....? (happen)
Nothing happened yesterday.
6 ....? (phone)
I phone him every week.

Past perfect

Affirmative		
I/He/She/It We/You/They	'd (had) escaped	by then.
Negative		
I/He/She/It We/You/They	hadn't (had not) escaped	by then.

Questions and short answers
Had I/he/she/it/we/you/they escaped by then? Yes, I/he/she/it/we/you/they had. No, I/he/she/it/we/you/they hadn't.

Wh- questions
Where had you escaped from?

Irregular verbs have different past participle forms. (See **Irregular verb list**, Workbook page 125).

Time expressions and sequencing words

after	already	before	by (+ a time)	by the
time	just	for	since	when

*He'd **just** put on his disguise **when** the phone rang.*
***By the time** the rain stopped, everyone had **already** gone.*
*We'd known them **for many years/since we were at primary school**.*

Use

We use the Past perfect to talk about actions or situations that happened:

- before a specific moment in the past.
  ***By the time he was twenty**, he'**d become** a famous detective.*
  *I'**d solved** the problem **by eight o'clock**.*

- before another action or situation in the past. We use the Past simple to talk about the later action or situation.
  *He'**d left** before I **arrived**.* (He left. Then I arrived.)
  *Before she **got** home, they'**d broken** into her house.* (They broke into her house. Then she got home.)

Form

We form the Past perfect with *had* + past participle:
*She'**d gone**.*
*I **hadn't gone**.*
***Had** they **gone**?*

Third conditional

Affirmative
If he'd (had) asked me for help, I'd (would) have helped him. They'd (would) have escaped if she'd (had) given them the key.

Negative
If he hadn't (had not) followed her, he wouldn't (would not) have discovered the truth. I wouldn't (would not) have been angry with you if you hadn't (had not) lied.

Questions
Would you have believed me if I'd (had) told you the truth? If he'd (had) seen the thief, what would he have done?

Use

We use the Third conditional to talk about unreal situations or events in the past (situations or events that did not happen).

If they'd listened to me, they'd have caught the spy. (They didn't listen to me, so they didn't catch the spy.)

I wouldn't have screamed if I hadn't been frightened. (I was frightened, so I screamed.)

Form

- To form the Third conditional, we use:
  if + Past perfect, *would(n't) have* + past participle
  ***If he'd run**, he **wouldn't have been** late.*
  OR
  would(n't) have + past participle + *if* + Past perfect
  *He **wouldn't have been** late **if he'd run**.*

- We can use the conditional clause (starting with *if*) and the result clause in any order, but we must use a comma when the conditional clause comes first.
  ***If I'd known**, I'd have helped.* = *I'd have helped if I'd known*.

- Remember: *had* and *would* can both be contracted to *'d*.
  *If I'**d (had)** known, I'**d (would)** have helped.*

Grammar practice

Past perfect

1 Complete the sentences with the Past perfect form of the verbs. Underline the action or event which happened first.

1 I arrived after the party *had finished* (finish).
2 We left after the film
   .... (start).
3 Belle .... (eat) lunch before she went shopping.
4 By the time he was ten, Tom
   .... (became) famous.
5 He .... (just/wake) up when the phone rang.
6 The robbery ....
   (already/happen) before we got home.

2 Choose the correct options.

1 They were late because they *stayed /* (*'d stayed*) too long at the café.
2 I*'d never seen / never saw* that woman before she appeared last night.
3 We *knew / 'd known* each other for years before I learnt the truth.
4 After we'd had lunch we *drank / 'd drunk* a coffee.
5 The concert still *didn't finish / hadn't finished* by eleven o'clock.
6 **A** Had they put on their disguises before they *left / 'd left*?
   B No, they *didn't / hadn't*.

3 Complete the sentences. Use a Past simple and a Past perfect form in each sentence.

1 She*'d studied* (study) French for years before she *moved* (move) to Paris.
2 After we .... (see) the menu, we .... (order) our meals.
3 They .... (just/sit) down when Max .... (appear).
4 By the time we .... (reach) the station, the train .... (already/leave).
5 I .... (want) to go to New York because I .... (never/be) there before.
6 I .... (not see) the film before, so I .... (decide) to buy a ticket.

Third conditional

4 Choose the correct options.

1 If I'd seen him, I (*'d have screamed*)/ *screamed*!
2 He would have caught the thief if he *ran / 'd run* a bit faster.
3 She would have reported him to the police if he *isn't / hadn't been* her brother.
4 If you'd locked the door, she *wouldn't get / wouldn't have got* in.
5 Would *you have stolen / have you stolen* the money if you'd found the purse?
6 If he *didn't commit / hadn't committed* a crime he wouldn't have gone to prison.

5 Complete the Third conditional sentences with the correct form of the verbs.

1 I*'d have passed* (pass) the law exam if I*'d worked* (work) harder.
2 He .... (escape) if he .... (not fall) over.
3 If I .... (not become) a detective, I .... (be) a spy.
4 If you .... (phone) the police, this .... (not happen).
5 What .... (you/do) if you .... (see) him?
6 If I .... (not help) you, who .... (you/ask)?

6 Write Third conditional sentences about these situations.

1 He was poor, so he took the money.
   If he hadn't *been poor*, he *wouldn't have taken the money*.
2 They didn't follow us, so we were safe.
   If they'd .... , we ....
3 She was in a hurry, so she didn't wait.
   If she hadn't .... , she ....
4 I hid because I was scared.
   I wouldn't .... if I ....
5 We didn't watch the film because we didn't have enough money.
   We'd .... if we ....
6 I knew what to do after I'd read his message.
   I wouldn't .... if I ....

Reported statements

Direct speech	Reported speech *I said/told her that … .*
Present simple → 'We dance.'	**Past simple** … we danced.
Present continuous → 'We're dancing.'	**Past continuous** … we were dancing.
Past simple → 'We danced.'	**Past perfect** … we'd danced.
Present perfect → 'We've danced.'	**Past perfect** … we'd danced.
am/is/are going to → 'We're going to dance.'	*was/were going to* … we were going to dance.
will/ won't → 'We'll dance.'	*would/wouldn't* … we would dance.
have to/must → 'We have to dance.' 'We must dance.'	*had to* … we had to dance.
can → 'We can dance.'	*could* … we could dance.

- When we report speech, we put the main verb one step back in time.
  *'I **broke** it.'* → *He said that he'**d broken** it.*
- We do not use inverted commas in reported speech.
- We report statements with *said that* or *told* + indirect object + *that*:
  *I **said that** it was OK. / I **told her that** it was OK.*
  NOT *I said her that it was OK. / I told that it was OK.*
- We often need to change pronouns and possessive adjectives.
  *'I've lost **my** keys,' she said.* →
  *She said that she'd lost **her** keys.*
- We often change expressions of time and place.
  *'I'll stay **here tonight**.'* →
  *He said that he would stay **there that night**.*

direct speech → reported speech
now → then   today/tonight → that day/that night
this week → that week   yesterday → the day before
last month → the month before
five years ago → five years before
tomorrow → the next day
next year → the following year   here → there

Reported commands and requests

Affirmative	
'Leave!' → 'Please leave.' →	He told us to leave. He asked us to leave.

Negative	
'Don't leave!' → 'Please don't leave.' →	He told us not to leave. He asked us not to leave.

- To report requests and commands, we use: subject + *asked/told* + object (+ *not*) + infinitive.
  *We **asked them to stay**.*
  *I **told her not to shout**.*
- We don't use *please* in reported requests.

Reported questions

Wh- questions	
'Who is she?' → 'When did it start?' →	I asked him who she was. She asked me when it had started.

Yes/No questions	
'Do you like me?' → 'Will you help us?' →	He asked me if I liked him. They asked us if we'd help them.

- We do not use question marks (?) in reported questions.
- Tenses change, and pronouns, possessive adjectives and time and place expressions often change. See **Reported statements** (above).
- Reported questions have the same word order as an affirmative sentence.
  *'Where **are you**?'* → *I asked her where **she was**.*
  NOT *I asked her where was she.*
- If a direct question uses question words (*who*, *what*, *how*, etc.), we repeat the same question words in the reported question.
  *'**How** are you?'* → *He asked me **how** I was.*
- If a direct question does NOT use question words (*who*, *what*, *how*, etc.), we use *if* in the reported question. We do not use *do/does/did*.
  'Do you know me?' → *She asked me **if** I knew her.*
  'Will you stay?' → *I asked her **if** she'd stay.*

Grammar practice

Reported statements

1 Write the correct reported speech form of the <u>underlined</u> verbs.

1 'I'<u>m throwing</u> a party!'
Dan told Ash that he *was throwing* a party.
2 'I <u>decorated</u> the house yesterday.'
Dan said that he .... the house the day before.
3 'I'<u>ve emailed</u> you an invitation.'
Dan told Ash that he .... her an invitation.
4 'I'<u>ll come</u>!'
Ash said that she ....
5 'I <u>can bring</u> some music.'
Ash told Dan that she .... some music.
6 'The party <u>is going to be</u> great!'
Dan said that the party .... great.

2 Read the direct speech. Then complete the reported sentences with the correct pronouns, possessive adjectives and time and place expressions.

'¹*I* had a great time at Olivia's party ²<u>last night</u>. She invited lots of people from ³<u>our</u> school. ⁴ I'm meeting some of them ⁵<u>here</u> later ⁶<u>today</u>.'

Nathan said that ¹*he*'d had a great time at Olivia's party ²....................... . He told Sophie that Olivia had invited lots of people from ³.......................
school. He explained that ⁴....................... was meeting some of them ⁵....................... later
⁶....................... .

3 Rewrite the sentences in reported speech.

1 Keira → Will: 'We met a year ago.'
Keira told *Will that they'd met the year before.*
2 I → them: 'I really enjoyed your party.'
I told ....
3 'I've never been here before.'
I said ....
4 Vicki → me: 'I'll call you next week.'
Vicki told ....
5 'We must go now.'
They said ....
6 Steve → Emma: 'I love your dress.'
Steve told ....

Reported commands and requests

4 Are these sentences commands (*C*) or requests (*R*)? Rewrite them in reported speech.

1 'Go away!' .*C*.
2 'Please come in.' ....
3 'Stop talking!' ....
4 'Please help.' ....
5 'Please don't go.' ....
6 'Don't sit there!' ....

1 She *told* me *to go away.*
2 I .... them ....
3 The teacher .... us
....
4 He .... me ....
5 I .... her ....
6 You .... him ....

Reported questions

5 Choose the correct options.

1 I asked her if *wanted she / (she wanted)* to come.
2 He asked me how *getting home I was / I was getting home.*
3 They asked her who the guests *will be / would be.*
4 She asked him *if / that* he could book a limo.
5 Mara asked you *did you like / if you liked* the music.
6 Tim asked us how long *had we been / we'd been* there.

6 Phil asks Layla a lot of questions at a party! Rewrite his questions in reported speech.

1 'Do you want to dance?'
He asked her if she wanted to dance.
2 'Have we met before?'
....
3 'Can I get you a drink?'
....
4 'Did I tell you about my heavy metal band?'
....
5 'Do you want to meet up tomorrow night?'
....
6 'Where are you going?'
....

Vocabulary 1

Different Lives

Unit vocabulary

1 Translate the words.

Compound nouns	
babysitter	....
businessperson	....
caretaker	....
classmate	....
homework	....
lighthouse	....
skyscraper	....
snowmobile	....
spaceship	....
speedboat	....
whiteboard	....
windmill	....

2 Translate the words.

Phrasal verbs 1	
fill in	....
find out	....
get back	....
give up	....
go away	....
hang out	....
look after	....
look for	....
run away	....
set up	....

Vocabulary extension

3 Match the photos to the compound nouns in the box. Use your dictionary if necessary. Write the words in English and your language.

~~headphones~~   lifeguard   motorway
playground   seatbelt   weightlifter

1 .... *headphones* ....

....

2 ....

....

3 ....

....

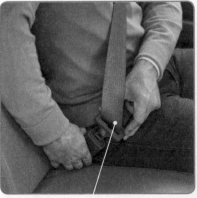

4 ....

....

5 ....

....

6 ....

....

Vocabulary 2

Aiming High

Unit vocabulary

1 Translate the expressions.

Collocations with *make*, *go* and *keep*

go abroad ....
go crazy ....
go for a walk ....
go missing ....
keep a secret ....
keep calm ....
keep control ....
keep in touch ....
make a decision ....
make a difference ....
make someone's dream come true ....
make it to the final ....

2 Translate the words.

Jobs and suffixes *-or*, *-er*, *-ist*

art ....
artist ....
novel ....
novelist ....
photograph ....
photographer ....
play ....
playwright ....
poem ....
poet ....
sculptor ....
sculpture ....

Vocabulary extension

3 Match the photos to the collocations in the box. Use your dictionary if necessary. Write the expressions in English and your language.

go on holiday	~~go shopping~~	keep a diary
keep fit	make a mistake	make friends

1 .... *go shopping* ....

2 ....

3 ....

4 ....

5 ....

6 ....

Vocabulary 3

Be Happy!

Unit vocabulary

1 Translate the words.

Showing feelings

blush ....
cry ....
frown ....
gasp ....
laugh ....
scream ....
shiver ....
shout ....
sigh ....
smile ....
sweat ....
yawn ....

2 Translate the words.

Adjective suffixes

beautiful ....
dangerous ....
famous ....
healthy ....
lucky ....
peaceful ....
poisonous ....
successful ....
wealthy ....

Vocabulary extension

3 Match the photos to the adjectives in the box. Use your dictionary if necessary. Write the words in English and your language.

annoyed   excited   jealous   proud   relaxed   ~~stressed~~

1 ....*stressed*............
....

2 ....
....

3 ....
....

4 ....
....

5 ....
....

6 ....
....

Vocabulary 4

Survive!

Unit vocabulary

1 Translate the words.

Natural disasters

Nouns

avalanche ....

cyclone ....

disease ....

drought ....

earthquake ....

famine ....

flood ....

tsunami ....

volcano ....

Verbs

bury ....

destroy ....

drown ....

erupt ....

spread ....

starve ....

survive ....

2 Translate the phrasal verbs.

Phrasal verbs 2

break down ....

calm down ....

come across ....

get through ....

keep on ....

look forward to ....

put on ....

run out of ....

take off ....

work out ....

Vocabulary extension

3 Match the pictures to the verbs in the box. Use your dictionary if necessary. Write the words in English and your language.

burn   crash   freeze   injure   rescue   ~~sink~~

1 ....*sink*...............

2 ....

3 ....

4 ....

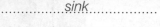

5 ....

6 ....

Vocabulary 5

Work For It

Unit vocabulary

1   Translate the words and expressions.

Work collocations

answer the phone   ....

attend a meeting   ....

check emails   ....

deal with enquiries   ....

do some photocopying   ....

give a presentation   ....

make an appointment   ....

order stationery   ....

prepare a spreadsheet   ....

take payments   ....

work on reception   ....

write a report   ....

2   Translate the words and expressions.

Job qualities

Adjectives

accurate   ....

analytical   ....

experienced   ....

organised   ....

patient   ....

practical   ....

punctual   ....

reliable   ....

Nouns and noun phrases

excellent IT skills   ....

good communicator   ....

leadership qualities   ....

team player   ....

Vocabulary extension

3   Match the objects in the picture to the words in the box. Use your dictionary if necessary. Write the words in English and your language.

file(s)   keyboard   monitor   noticeboard   photocopier   printer

1 .... file(s) ....

2 ....

3 ....

4 ....

5 ....

6 ....

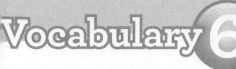

Vocabulary 6

Coast

Unit vocabulary

1 Translate the words.

Coastal life

amusement arcade ....

beach hut ....

cliffs ....

deckchair ....

fish and chip shop ....

go-karts ....

harbour ....

ice cream kiosk ....

pier ....

seagull ....

sea wall ....

souvenir shop ....

2 Translate the words.

Verbs with prefixes *re-* and *dis-*

disagree ....

disappear ....

discontinue ....

discover ....

dislike ....

recover ....

release ....

remove ....

replace ....

research ....

restore ....

Vocabulary extension

3 Match the photos to the words in the box. Use your dictionary if necessary. Write the words in English and your language.

| beach volleyball | fishing | kayaking |
| ~~sailing~~ | scuba-diving | sunbathing |

1 .... *sailing* ....

....

2 ....

....

3 ....

....

4 ....

....

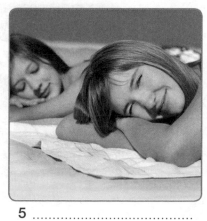

5 ....

....

6 ....

....

Final Frontiers

Unit vocabulary

1 Translate the words.

Adjective antonyms

ancient ....
modern .... (opp.)

dark ....
light .... (opp.)

deep ....
shallow .... (opp.)

heavy ....
light .... (opp.)

low ....
high .... (opp.)

narrow ....
wide .... (opp.)

ordinary ....
strange .... (opp.)

temporary ....
permanent .... (opp.)

weak ....
powerful .... (opp.)
strong .... (opp.)

2 Translate the words.

Space

asteroid ....
astronaut ....
astronomer ....
comet ....
galaxy ....
Moon ....
orbit ....
planet ....
solar system ....
spacecraft ....
star ....
telescope ....

Vocabulary extension

3 Match the pictures to the pairs of adjective antonyms
(e.g. *ancient/modern*) in the box. Use your dictionary if
necessary. Write the words in English and your language.

asleep   awake   dry   empty   full   ~~wet~~

1 ....wet.............. 2 ....
....

3 .... 4 ....
....

5 .... 6 ....
....

Spies

Unit vocabulary

1 Translate the words and expressions.

Spy collocations

break into somewhere

....

decode a message

....

escape from somewhere

....

follow someone ....

make a deal ....

spy on someone ....

take cover ....

tap a phone ....

tell a lie ....

tell the truth ....

track down a person

....

wear a disguise ....

2 Translate the words.

Adjectives with prefixes *dis-*, *im-*, *in-*, *un-*

dishonest ....

disloyal ....

dissatisfied ....

impatient ....

impolite ....

impossible ....

inappropriate ....

incorrect ....

intolerant ....

unfair ....

unimportant ....

unsuccessful ....

Vocabulary extension

3 Match the pictures to the spy collocations in the box. Use your dictionary if necessary. Write the collocations in English and your language.

do some research	~~look for clues~~	make notes
report a crime to the police	solve a crime	take photos

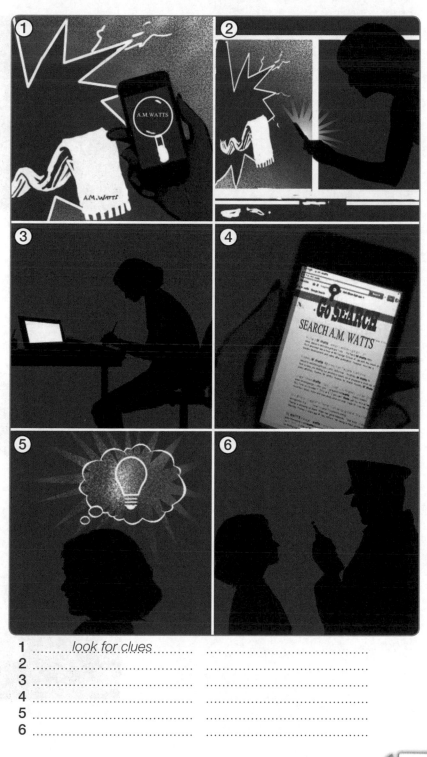

1 ....*look for clues*........... ....

2 ....

3 ....

4 ....

5 ....

6 ....

Celebrate!

Unit vocabulary

1 Translate the expressions.

Party collocations

do your hair ....

greet your guests ....

have the time of your life

....

hire a DJ ....

make a speech ....

put up decorations ....

stay up all night ....

throw a party ....

travel by limo ....

wear a jacket and tie

....

wear casual clothes

....

wear high heels ....

wear smart clothes ....

2 Translate the words.

Reporting verbs

verb + object (+ *not*) + infinitive

invite ....

warn ....

verb (+ *not*) + infinitive

agree ....

offer ....

promise ....

refuse ....

verb + *that* + reported statement

admit ....

complain ....

explain ....

mention ....

Vocabulary extension

3 Match the photos to the celebration and party collocations in the box. Use your dictionary if necessary. Write the collocations in English and your language.

go to a wedding	have a barbecue	open presents
~~send invitations~~	set off fireworks	watch a parade

1 ....*send invitations*........
....

2 ....
....

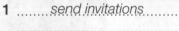

3 ....
....

4 ....
....

5 ....
....

6 ....
....

Expressing extremes

Speaking

1 🔊 32 **Choose the correct options. Then listen and check.**

1 A I'm (so) / *such* tired! I've had *so / such* a hard day.
 B Well, sit down and I'll make you a cup of tea.

2 A Max has really changed, hasn't he?
 B Definitely! He used to be *such / really* shy. Now he's *such / so* friendly.

3 A How was your holiday?
 B Great! We had *so / such* a good time. Seville is *really / such* beautiful.

2 🔊 33 **Complete the conversation with these phrases. Then listen and check.**

really easy	really hungry	so difficult
so good	~~so sad~~	such a bad
such a good		

Rufus Hey, Mira, what's up? Why do you look ¹ *so sad*?

Mira Oh, hey Rufus. I'm having ² .... day. I've just had my first moped lesson. I was terrible! It was ³ ....

Rufus Don't worry. After a few weeks' it'll seem ⁴ .... You'll be fine!

Mira Thanks, Rufus. You're ⁵ .... friend. You always say the right thing!

Rufus Let's go to Rosa's Café. I'm ⁶ .... , and the cakes at Rosa's are ⁷ .... you'll soon feel better.

Listening

3 🔊 34 **Listen to the conversation. Match the people (1–5) to the names (a–e).**

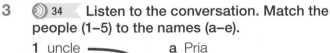

1 uncle   a Pria
2 friend   b Lottie Field
3 sister   c Ellis
4 grandmother   d Kayleigh
5 niece   e Charlotte West

4 🔊 34 **Listen again. Complete the sentences. Write between one and two words in each gap.**

1 Ellis says the news makes him feel *really old*.
2 Pria thinks the baby's got such .... name.
3 Ellis's sister named the baby after ....
4 The picture on Ellis's phone isn't very good because the baby was ....
5 Pria thinks that Ellis and the baby have got similar ....
6 Ellis doesn't want to be .... until the baby is older.

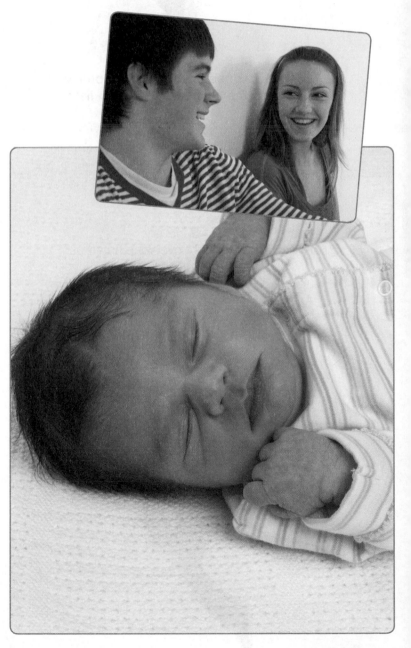

Speaking and Listening 2

Giving/Responding to news

Speaking

1 🔊 35 **Choose the correct options to complete the conversation. Then listen and check.**

Arthur What's ¹ *on / up*, Jess?

Jess I've ² *just / now* heard some amazing news! You won't ³ *believe / think* it, but we've made it to the finals of the dance competition!

Arthur ⁴ *Not / No* way!

Jess ⁵ *Serious / Seriously.*

Arthur But I thought everyone hated us! ⁶ *What's / How's* the story?

Jess Well, we were wrong! They loved us!

Arthur ⁷ *Believable / Unbelievable.*

Jess And I've got even more good news … we've won a prize of £50!

Arthur You ⁸ *kid / 're kidding* me! Wow.

2 🔊 36 **Complete the conversations. Write one word in each gap. Then listen and check.**

1 A What's *up*, Josh? Are you OK?

  B I'm OK, thanks. But I've .... heard some sad news.

2 A I got 100% in my exam!

  B No .... ! You're kidding me.

  A Seriously. I swear it's ....

3 A You .... believe it, but something amazing has just happened.

  B ....'s the story?

Listening

3 🔊 37 **Listen to the conversation. What's the main piece of news for Barney and Scarlett?**

a They aren't going on holiday this year. ☐

b They're now millionaire lottery winners. ☐

c They're going on an exciting holiday. ☐

4 🔊 37 **Listen again. Choose the best options.**

1 *Dad / Barney* phoned *Dad / Barney*.

2 Scarlett is reading a *book / magazine*.

3 Last summer Barney and Scarlett went to *Cornwall / France / California*.

4 This year, Barney and Scarlett are going to *Cornwall / France / California*.

5 Dad has already paid for the *hotel rooms / plane tickets*.

6 Dad *won / didn't win* a lottery prize.

Invitations

Speaking

1 🔊 38 **Put the words in the correct order. Then listen and check.**

1 A *Do you want to meet us at the café?*
meet / you / us / want / Do / to / at the café / to / ?

B OK, thanks. ....
you / I'll / there / see

2 A ....
shopping / fancy / going / Do / you / ?

B Sorry. ....
say / going to / I'm / no / have to

3 A ....
you / play / Would / basketball / like / to / ?

B ....
fun, / That / I'm afraid / sounds / I /
can't, / but

2 🔊 39 **Complete the conversation with these words and phrases. Then listen and check.**

~~fancy~~	great	I'd	I'll
'm afraid	like	Sorry	want

Nell Do you [1] *fancy* going for a bike ride tomorrow?

Tom That sounds fun, but I can't,
I [2] .... I haven't got a bike.

Nell Well, would you [3] .... to go swimming?

Tom [4] .... I'm going to have to say no. I hate swimming!

Nell OK. Do you [5] .... to play video games, as usual?

Tom That's a [6] .... idea.
[7] .... love to. But let's meet at my house. Come round at 12.00 and I'll make you lunch.

Nell OK, thanks. [8] .... see you there!

Listening

3 🔊 40 **Listen to the phone conversations. Answer the questions. Use names from the box.**

Alice	Bethany	Dan	Mark	Tessa

1 Who does Mark phone?
Bethany, Dan and Alice

2 Who really likes Tessa?
....

3 Who's tired?
....

4 Who's visiting grandparents?
....

5 Who's going on the picnic?
.... , ... ,
.... , and ....

4 🔊 40 **Listen again. Complete the information about the picnic.**

1 Day: *Saturday*
2 Place: ....
3 Time: ....
4 Food: .... , ...
and ....
5 Drink: .... and ....

Asking for clarification

Speaking

1 🔊 41 **Choose the correct options. Then listen and check.**

Nina You ¹*should don't wear /* ⟨*shouldn't wear*⟩ that T-shirt!

Pippa What ²*do you mean / are you meaning*? ³*Do you say / Are you saying* that you don't like this T-shirt?

Nina No, but it's the wrong colour for walking in the desert.

Pippa Sorry, I ⁴*don't understand / haven't been understanding*. Why is it wrong?

Nina Well, black keeps you warm. You should wear white or a light colour to keep cool.

Pippa Oh, ⁵*I've seen / I see*! Thanks. I'll find another one …

2 🔊 42 **Complete the conversation. Write one word in each gap. Then listen and check.**

Lara You ¹*should* take suncream and sunglasses if you're walking in the Alps in winter.

Oli Sorry, I ²......................... understand. Are you ³......................... that the Alps will be *hot* in January?

Lara No, but you'll need suncream!

Oli What ⁴......................... ⁵......................... mean?

Lara Well, the sun on the snow is very bright. Your skin might burn.

Oli ⁶........................., I see! Thanks.

Listening

3 🔊 43 **Listen to the conversation and answer the questions.**

1 Why does Polly want to stop? Choose *two* reasons. She's …
   a tired. ☐   **b** cold. ☐   **c** hungry. ☐

2 Which places do Bart and Polly visit? Choose *two*.
   a a river ☐   **b** a field ☐   **c** a wood ☐

3 What problems do Bart and Polly have? Choose *two*.

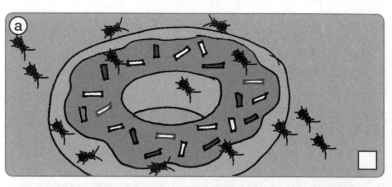

4 🔊 43 **Listen again and complete the sentences.**

1 Polly wants to stop *walking*.

2 Polly thinks that the .... is very pretty.

3 Polly and Bart reach the field .... minutes later.

4 .... sees the café first.

5 .... doesn't think they should go in the café.

6 .... thinks the café will be a nice place to eat because it hasn't got ....

Phone language

Speaking

1))) 44 **Complete the conversations. Write one word in each gap. Then listen and check.**

1 A *My* name's Eloise Power. I'd .... to speak to the manager, please.
B I'll pass you .... to him. Just a moment.

2 A Hello. I'm John Clarke. .... I speak to Mr Calvino, please?
B I'll put you through now. Hold .... , please.

3 A Hi. I'm Katie Matthews. I'm calling .... the cleaning job.
B I'm afraid the manager isn't here right now. Can I .... a message?

2))) 45 **Complete the conversation with these words and phrases. Then listen and check.**

I'll pass	I'll put	I'm calling about
~~my name's~~	I speak to	I take

Assistant	Stu's Sports.
Maya	Hello. ¹*My name's* Maya Smith. ² .... the weekend job which you advertised in *Sports Times*. Can ³ .... Elaine Flannigan, please?
Assistant	⁴ .... you through now. Hold on, please. I'm very sorry. Elaine isn't here, but you can speak to our assistant manager, Wayne. ⁵ .... you over to him. Just a moment.
Wayne	Hi there, Wayne Hudson here. Can ⁶ .... a message? I'll pass it on to Elaine when she gets back.

Listening

3))) 46 **Listen to two phone conversations. Write *Lydia*, *Steve*, *both* or *neither*.**

Who:
1 is phoning the *May Art Gallery*?   *both*
2 wants to speak to Mrs May?   ....
3 leaves a message with the receptionist? ....
4 is definitely going to an interview on Saturday? ....
5 has just started a new job at the information desk?   ....

4))) 46 **Listen again. Is the information below correct (✓) or incorrect (✗)? Correct any mistakes.**

Phone call A
1 Caller's first name: Lidia   ✗   *Lydia*
2 Caller's surname: Briteman   ....
3 Time of interview: 10.45   ....

Phone call B
4 Time Mrs May returns from lunch: 1:30   ....
5 Caller's phone number: 01125 463979   ....
6 Time the gallery closes on Sunday: 5.00   ....

Speaking and Listening 6

Asking for and giving directions

Speaking

1 🔊 47 **Look at the maps and complete the conversations. Listen and check.**

1 A Excuse me, could you tell me where the museum is?
B Go *past* the bookshop and then turn ....

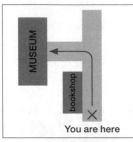

2 A Excuse me, could you direct me to the .... ?
B Take the .... turning on the right. You'll see it!

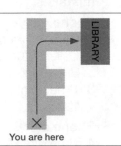

3 A Excuse me, how do I get to the station?
B Take the .... left. It's on the ....

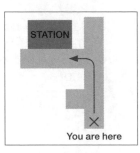

2 🔊 48 **Choose the best options. Then listen and check.**

Miguel ¹.... me, could you ².... me to the police station?

Woman Yes, of course. Turn right out ³.... here. When you see the bank, ⁴.... over the road. Go ⁵.... the pharmacy and then ⁶.... right. It's ⁷.... the left. You can't ⁸.... it.

1 **a** Sorry **b** Afraid **c** Excuse
2 **a** direct **b** send **c** tell
3 **a** of **b** to **c** away
4 **a** take **b** cross **c** turn
5 **a** pass **b** passed **c** past
6 **a** take **b** turn **c** make
7 **a** at **b** on **c** about
8 **a** lose **b** notice **c** miss

Listening

3 🔊 49 **Listen to three conversations. Which places do you hear?**

1 fish and chip shop ✓
2 aquarium
3 post office
4 sea wall
5 church
6 harbour
7 ice cream kiosk
8 bank
9 souvenir shop
10 beach
11 art gallery
12 pier

4 🔊 49 **Listen again and complete the table.**

How long is the journey?		
Journey 1	¹ *ten* minutes	
Journey 2	² .... minutes	
Journey 3	³ .... minutes	
What should the visitors do?		
Journey 1	Order ⁴ .... with fish and chips.	
Journey 2	Watch the ⁵ .... eating.	
Journey 3	Take photos of the colourful ⁶	

Giving warnings

Speaking

1 🔊 **50** **Match the sentences (1–6) with the replies (a–f) to complete the conversations. Then listen and check.**

1 We're going up the mountain.   *e*
2 I'm going to try to jump across the river.
3 We're going to pick mushrooms.
4 I'm going to put my tent here.
5 I'm going to apologise.

a Watch out for the poisonous ones!
b Be careful not to fall in!
c OK. But be careful not to upset her!
d I wouldn't camp on the beach if I were you.
e Watch out for falling rocks!

2 🔊 **51** **Complete the conversation. Write one or two words in each gap. Then listen and check.**

Joy I'm going to my first music festival next weekend! Any advice?
Ali Make ¹*sure* you don't arrive late.
Leah Yes, and be careful ² .... lose your ticket! You're *so* forgetful.
Zoe Watch ³ .... thieves! I wouldn't take too much money if ⁴ .... you.
Xavier Oh, and ⁵ .... sure you ⁶ .... forget to text us!

Listening

3 🔊 **52** **Listen to the conversation. Match the locations (1–6) to the items (a–f).**

1 in the wardrobe   *f*
2 on the chair   ....
3 in a drawer   ....
4 on a small table   ....
5 under the bed   ....
6 on the desk   ....

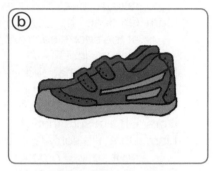
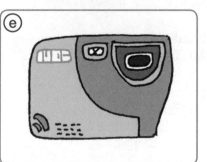
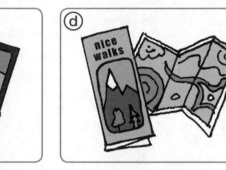

4 🔊 **52** **Listen again. Answer the questions.**

1 Who is talking?
   Freya and her mum.
2 Why is her mum annoyed?
   Freya's only just .... for her holiday.
3 What kind of trip is Freya going on?
   A ....
4 What does she want to borrow?
   A ....
5 What *doesn't* Freya's mum think she should take?
   A ....
6 Why?
   She thinks it's .... and Freya .... it.

Explaining and apologising

Speaking

1 🔊 **53** **Choose the best options. Then listen and check.**

Dora Liam! I'm really mad with you. ¹.... did you take my bike?

Liam Oh dear. The ².... is that I was late for work at the sports centre. If I arrive late, I might lose my job!

Dora I'm ³.... of that. But you should ask!

Liam I know ⁴.... . You have to ⁵.... that I was in a hurry, and I couldn't find you. I did try!

Dora Oh, I'm sure that's ⁶.... .

Liam Dora, I'm sorry ⁷.... I took your bike. I won't do it again, I promise.

Dora Oh, let's ⁹.... about it. It's kind of funny anyway. I bet everyone at work laughed when you arrived on a pink bike!

1	**a** How	**b** Why		**c** What	
2	**a** fact	**b** story		**c** reality	
3	**a** awake	**b** knowing		**c** aware	
4	**a** this	**b** that		**c** it	
5	**a** see	**b** know		**c** understand	
6	**a** true	**b** so		**c** certain	
7	**a** about	**b** that		**c** for	
8	**a** lose	**b** stop		**c** forget	

2 🔊 **54** **Complete the conversations. Write one or two words in each gap. Then listen and check.**

1 A I'm so ¹ *sorry* that I upset you. I didn't realise that you were scared of spiders!

B Oh, I'm sure ² .... true. I know it was just a joke. ³ .... forget about it, OK?

2 A Why won't you let me go to the party! The fact ⁴ .... you don't trust me.

B No, that's not true. But ⁵ .... to understand that we're your parents …

A I'm aware ⁶ .... !

B I hadn't finished! We're your parents, so we worry.

Listening

3 🔊 **55** **Listen to the conversation. Then answer the questions. Write C (Chloë) or J (Jason).**

Who:
1 expresses anger?   *J*
2 explains why they did something bad?   ....
3 is worried about something?   ....
4 apologises?   ....
5 offers help?   ....
6 makes an invitation?   ....

4 🔊 **55** **Listen again. Are the sentences true (T), false (F) or don't know (DK)?**

1 When Jason arrives, Chloë is looking at his books.   *T*
2 Chloë is copying Jason's French homework.   ....
3 Chloë is worried about Chemistry.   ....
4 Chloë failed most of her exams last time.   ....
5 Jason never asks for help with school subjects.   ....
6 Chloë and Jason are meeting at the weekend.   ....
7 Chloë usually wins computer games.   ....

Reaching an agreement
Speaking

1 🔊 56 **Put the words in the correct order. Then listen and check.**

1 A *I think we should go home.*
  go / home / I / should / think / we
  B No way! The party's just getting started!

2 A ....
  don't / Why / walk / we / there / ?
  B That makes sense.

3 A ....
  can / Maybe / make / we / decorations / some
  B I agree. I think we should have a Halloween theme!

4 A ....
  stay / Do / think / you / with Ava / we / could / ?
  B ....
  good / a / idea / That's
  I'll ask her.

2 🔊 57 **Complete the conversation with these words and phrases. Then listen and check.**

a good idea	could	don't we	~~maybe~~
sense	should	think	way

Mary How are we going to get to the festival? [1] *Maybe* we can get a train.
Heath That's [2] .... , but it's quite a long walk from the station. Do you think your brother [3] .... give us a lift?
Mary I don't think we [4] .... ask him! He's a terrible driver. Why [5] .... get a taxi?
Heath No [6] .... ! A taxi would be really expensive. I [7] .... we should get a bus, and save our money for food, drink and band T-shirts.
Mary That makes [8] .... Let's do that.

Listening

3 🔊 58 **Listen to the conversation. Number the activities in the order that you hear them.**

4 🔊 58 **Listen again. Choose the correct options.**

1 When is Ellie's birthday?
  a 10th   **b** 16th   **c** 21st

2 What *didn't* happen to Ellie this month?
  a Her dog died.
  b She failed her moped test.
  c She lost a singing contest.

3 Who likes karaoke?
  a Kev   **b** Aisha   **c** Blake

4 What kind of film *doesn't* Ellie like?
  a comedy   **b** fantasy   **c** horror

5 Who works at the restaurant?
  a A friend from school.
  b Blake.
  c Someone in Blake's family.

Pronunciation

Consonants

Symbol	Example	Your examples
/p/	pen	
/b/	book	
/t/	tea	
/d/	desk	
/k/	cat	
/g/	girl	
/tʃ/	cheese	
/dʒ/	June	
/f/	five	
/v/	very	
/θ/	thin	
/ð/	then	
/s/	so	
/z/	zoo	
/ʃ/	she	
/ʒ/	usually	
/h/	hat	
/m/	man	
/n/	now	
/ŋ/	thing	
/l/	long	
/r/	red	
/j/	yes	
/w/	week	

Vowels

Symbol	Example	Your examples
/ɪ/	sit	
/e/	ten	
/æ/	black	
/ɒ/	hot	
/ʌ/	up	
/ʊ/	full	
/iː/	see	
/eɪ/	pay	
/aɪ/	why	
/ɔɪ/	enjoy	
/uː/	too	
/əʊ/	home	
/aʊ/	loud	
/ɪə/	year	
/eə/	wear	
/ɑː/	far	
/ɔː/	four	
/ʊə/	sure	
/ɜː/	bird	
/i/	coffee	
/ə/	ago	
/u/	usually	

Pronunciation Practice

Unit 1 Compound noun word stress

1 ◗) 59 **Listen and repeat. Then mark the main stress in each word. Answer the question below.**

1 babysitter   4 skyscraper
2 caretaker   5 snowmobile
3 classmate   6 windmill

Do we usually stress the *first*, *second* or *last* syllable in compound nouns? ....

2 ◗) 60 **Mark the main stress. Then listen, check your answers and repeat.**

1 bedroom   4 hairdresser
2 blackboard   5 supermarket
3 notebook   6 newspaper

Unit 2 Sentence stress

1 ◗) 61 **Listen and repeat. Then mark the most stressed words.**

1 We're happy because we made it to the finals.
2 Can you help me? My dog has gone missing!
3 You've made our dreams come true.

> **Brain Trainer: sentence stress**
>
> We usually stress the most important content words in sentences (often main verbs, nouns and adjectives).
>
> Now do Exercise 2.

2 ◗) 62 **Mark the *three* most important content words in each sentence. Then listen, check your answers, and repeat the sentences, copying the stress.**

1 I've made a very big decision.
2 My sister has moved to France.
3 We went for a walk in the park.
4 Have you heard the news? I'm so excited!

Unit 3 Showing feelings

1 ◗) 63 **Listen. You hear a speaker say 'Did you see that?' in four different conversations. Is the speaker *afraid*, *angry*, *bored* or *excited*?**

1 ....   3 ....
2 ....   4 ....

2 ◗) 64 **Read the sentences. Do you think the speakers will sound *afraid*, *angry*, *bored* or *excited*? Listen, check your answers, and repeat, copying the intonation.**

1 I've won the lottery!
2 There's nothing to do here.
3 What's that noise?
4 Never lie to me again!

Unit 4 Consonant clusters

1 ◗) 65 **Listen and repeat. Do the <u>underlined</u> letters have *one*, *two* or *three* consonant sounds?**

a <u>squ</u>are   he<u>lps</u>   e<u>xp</u>ensive
b wea<u>th</u>er   <u>wh</u>ite   si<u>ck</u>
c buil<u>d</u>ing   ti<u>met</u>able fini<u>sh</u>ed

2 ◗) 66 **<u>Underline</u> the consonant clusters. Then listen and repeat.**

1 The bus stops on a quiet street.
2 I remember her lovely home in the country.
3 He found her passport in the suitcase.

Unit 5 /ɜː/ and /ɔː/

1 ◗) 67 **Listen and repeat. Then <u>underline</u> the sounds /ɜː/ or /ɔː/.**

/ɜː/ learn   third   dessert
/ɔː/ warm   before   thought

2 ◗) 68 **Complete the table. Then listen, check your answers, and repeat.**

<u>au</u>tumn   c<u>augh</u>t   <u>ear</u>ly   fl<u>oor</u>
j<u>our</u>ney   s<u>or</u>t   univ<u>er</u>sity w<u>or</u>ld

/ɜː/	/ɔː/
....	....
....	....
....	....
....	....

Pronunciation

Unit 6 Weak vs strong form of *was*

1 🔊 69   Listen and repeat, paying attention to the strong and weak forms of *was*. Then answer the question below.

A Are you cold?

B I **was** (/wɒz/), but I'm warmer now. It **was** (/wəz/) freezing earlier!

A The pier **was** (/wəz/) closed.

B **Was** (/wɒz/) it? Why?

Do we say /wɒz/ or /wəz/ when we want to emphasise *was*?   ....

2 🔊 70   Do you think the speaker will use strong (*S*) or weak (*W*) forms of the words in bold? Listen, check your answers, and repeat.

A The beach party [1] **was** (........................) amazing.

B [2] **Was** (........................) Bart there?

A Yes, he [3] **was** (........................)! He [4] **was** (........................) the DJ.

B [5] **Was** (........................) he? Wow. He used to be really shy.

A Yes, he [6] **was** (........................) shy before. But he isn't now!

Unit 7 Elided syllables

1 🔊 71   Listen and repeat. Write the number of syllables you hear (1, 2, 3). Then cross out the silent syllables (the letters that you *don't* hear).

1 listening   ....
2 average   ....
3 memory   ....
4 musically   ....

2 🔊 72   Cross out the silent syllables in the bold words. Then listen, check your answers, and repeat.

1 He worked for **several businesses**, but the work made him **miserable**.

2 My main **interests** are **literature** and photography. I've got three **cameras**!

3 **Every evening** we went to a **different restaurant**.

Unit 8 /eə/, /iː/, /eɪ/

1 🔊 73   Listen and repeat. Match the headings (a–c) to the columns (1–3) in the table.

a /eə/ (w**ear**) **b** /iː/ (d**eal**) **c** /eɪ/ (br**ea**k)

1	2	3 ....
t**ea**m	gr**ea**t	b**ear**
s**ea**t	st**ea**k	p**ear**

2 🔊 74   Which word does *not* include the sound? Listen and check your answers.

1 /eə/ squ**are**   st**air**   st**ay**
2 /iː/ p**ea**ch   p**eo**ple   p**air**
3 /eɪ/ m**ai**n   m**e**tre   mist**a**ke
4 /eə/ **a**ge   **air**port   anywh**ere**
5 /iː/ sc**a**red   s**e**cret   sp**ea**k
6 /eɪ/ w**ai**ter   w**ea**k   w**ei**ght

Unit 9 /ʃ/, /ʒ/, /dʒ/

⚙ **Brain Trainer: spelling /ʃ/, /ʒ/, /dʒ/**

We can spell the sounds /ʃ/, /ʒ/ and /dʒ/ in different ways. For example, we can write /ʃ/ as *sh* (*show*), *s* (*sure*), *ci* (*delicious*), *ti* (*pronunciation*), etc.

Now do Exercises 1 and 2.

1 🔊 75   Listen and repeat. Write the missing letters to complete the words.

/ʃ/	/ʒ/	/dʒ/
wa**sh**	A**si**a	fri**dge**
[1].....ugar	[3] u.....ually	[5].....uice
[2] spe.....al	[4] deci.....on	[6] langua.....

2 🔊 76   Match the words in bold (1–7) to the sounds (a–c). Then listen and check your answers.

a /ʃ/ **b** /ʒ/ **c** /dʒ/

A I [1] **should** (.....) make some [2] **introductions** (.....) … Nellie, this is Martin.

B It's a [3] **pleasure** (.....) to meet you, Martin. I like your [4] **jacket** (.....)! It's quite [5] **unusual** (.....).

C Thanks! Listen, Nellie, this might sound [6] **strange** (.....), but are you [7] **sure** (.....) we haven't met before?

Irregular Verb List

Verb	Past Simple	Past Participle
be	was/were	been
become	became	become
begin	began	begun
break	broke	broken
bring	brought	brought
build	built	built
buy	bought	bought
can	could	been able
catch	caught	caught
choose	chose	chosen
come	came	come
cost	cost	cost
cut	cut	cut
do	did	done
draw	drew	drawn
drink	drank	drunk
drive	drove	driven
eat	ate	eaten
fall	fell	fallen
feed	fed	fed
feel	felt	felt
fight	fought	fought
find	found	found
fly	flew	flown
forget	forgot	forgotten
get	got	got
give	gave	given
go	went	gone/been
have	had	had
hear	heard	heard
hold	held	held
keep	kept	kept
know	knew	known
learn	learned/learnt	learned/learnt
leave	left	left
lend	lent	lent

Verb	Past Simple	Past Participle
light	lit	lit
lose	lost	lost
make	made	made
mean	meant	meant
meet	met	met
pay	paid	paid
put	put	put
read /riːd/	read /red/	read /red/
ride	rode	ridden
ring	rang	rung
run	ran	run
say	said	said
see	saw	seen
sell	sold	sold
send	sent	sent
shine	shone	shone
show	showed	shown
sing	sang	sung
sit	sat	sat
sleep	slept	slept
speak	spoke	spoken
spell	spelled/spelt	spelled/spelt
spend	spent	spent
stand	stood	stood
steal	stole	stolen
swim	swam	swum
take	took	taken
teach	taught	taught
tell	told	told
think	thought	thought
throw	threw	thrown
understand	understood	understood
wake	woke	woken
wear	wore	worn
win	won	won
write	wrote	written

My Assessment Profile Starter Unit

1 **What can I do? Tick (✓) the options in the table.**

⏪ = I need to study this again.　　⏸ = I'm not sure about this.　　▶ = I'm happy with this.　　⏩ = I do this very well.

		⏪	⏸	▶	⏩
Grammar (Student's Book pages 4–7)	• I can use all forms of *be* and *have got* in the Present simple. • I can use all forms of the Present simple and Present continuous and understand when to use each tense. • I can use apostrophes, pronouns and possessive adjectives correctly. • I can make comparisons using comparative and superlative adjectives, *too* and *enough*. • I can use relative pronouns in defining relative clauses. • I can talk about quantity using *some*, *any*, *much*, *many* and *a lot of*. • I can use regular and irregular forms of the Past simple.				
Vocabulary (SB pages 4–7)	• I can talk about daily routines, free-time activities and feelings. • I can use different adjectives correctly. • I can tell the time.				
Listening (SB page 8)	• I can understand a conversation between friends.				
Speaking (SB page 8)	• I can ask for and give information about other people.				
Reading (SB page 9)	• I can understand an informal email giving news.				
Writing (SB page 9)	• I can write a description of a friend.				

2 **What new words and expressions can I remember?**

words　.........................　.........................　.........................　.........................　.........................　.........................

expressions　.........................　.........................　.........................　.........................

3 **How can I practise other new words and expressions?**

record them on my MP3 player ☐　　write them in a notebook ☐

practise them with a friend ☐　　translate them into my language ☐

4 **What English have I learned outside class?**

	words	expressions
on the radio		
in songs		
in films		
on the internet		
on TV		
with friends		

My Assessment Profile Unit 1

1 What can I do? Tick (✓) the options in the table.

⏪ = I need to study this again. ⏸ = I'm not sure about this. ▶ = I'm happy with this. ⏩ = I do this very well.

		⏪	⏸	▶	⏩
Vocabulary (Student's Book pages 10 and 13)	• I can form and use compound nouns to talk about jobs, transport, school and buildings. • I can understand and use ten phrasal verbs.				
Pronunciation (SB page 10)	• I can use the correct stress in compound nouns.				
Reading (SB pages 11 and 16)	• I can read and understand an article about different people's daily lives and an article about a man with an unusual job.				
Grammar (SB pages 12 and 15)	• I can understand when to use the Past simple or the Past continuous. • I can use the Past simple and the Past continuous in sentences using *when* and *while*. • I can use all forms of *used to* to talk about past habits.				
Speaking (SB page 14)	• I can express extremes using *so*, *such* and *really*.				
Listening (SB pages 14 and 16)	• I can understand a conversation between friends and a radio programme.				
Writing (SB page 17)	• I can use a variety of past tenses correctly. • I can write a short story.				

2 What new words and expressions can I remember?

words ....

expressions ....

3 How can I practise other new words and expressions?

record them on my MP3 player ☐ write them in a notebook ☐

practise them with a friend ☐ translate them into my language ☐

4 What English have I learned outside class?

	words	expressions
on the radio		
in songs		
in films		
on the internet		
on TV		
with friends		

My Assessment Profile Unit 2

1 What can I do? Tick (✓) the options in the table.

⏪ = I need to study this again.　⏸ = I'm not sure about this.　▶ = I'm happy with this.　⏩ = I do this very well.

		⏪	⏸	▶	⏩
Vocabulary (Student's Book pages 20 and 23)	• I can understand and use twelve collocations with *make*, *go* and *keep*. • I can form words for talking about jobs with *-er*, *-or*, *-ist* and other suffixes.				
Pronunciation (SB page 20)	• I can use the correct stress in sentences.				
Reading (SB pages 21 and 26)	• I can read and understand an article about an unusual football team and an article about two very successful people.				
Grammar (SB pages 22 and 25)	• I can use the Present perfect with *ever, never, already, yet* and *just* correctly. • I can use the Present perfect with *for* and *since* correctly. • I can understand when to use the Present perfect or the Past simple.				
Speaking (SB page 24)	• I can give and respond to news.				
Listening (SB pages 24 and 26)	• I can understand a conversation between friends and a news programme.				
Writing (SB page 27)	• I can use different time expressions. • I can write a biography.				

2 What new words and expressions can I remember?

words ....

expressions ....

3 How can I practise other new words and expressions?

record them on my MP3 player ☐　　write them in a notebook ☐
practise them with a friend ☐　　translate them into my language ☐

4 What English have I learned outside class?

	words	expressions
on the radio		
in songs		
in films		
on the internet		
on TV		
with friends		

My Assessment Profile Unit 3

1   What can I do? Tick (✓) the options in the table.

⏮ = I need to study this again.   ⏸ = I'm not sure about this.   ▶ = I'm happy with this.   ⏭ = I do this very well.

		⏮	⏸	▶	⏭
Vocabulary (Student's Book pages 30 and 33)	• I can talk about feelings and the way we express them. • I can form adjectives from nouns using the suffixes -*ful*, -*ous* and -*y*.				
Pronunciation (SB page 30)	• I can use intonation to express anger, boredom, excitement and fear.				
Reading (SB pages 31 and 36)	• I can read and understand an article about smiling and an article about two different views of fame.				
Grammar (SB pages 32 and 35)	• I can use gerunds after certain verbs and prepositions and as the subject or object of a sentence. • I can use infinitives after certain verbs and adjectives and to express purpose. • I can use the Present perfect continuous to talk about longer actions which started in the past and continue until the present.				
Speaking (SB pages 34–35)	• I can make and respond to invitations.				
Listening (SB pages 34–35 and 36)	• I can understand a conversation between friends and a radio interview.				
Writing (SB page 37)	• I can add and contrast ideas using linking words. • I can write a 'for and against' essay.				

2   What new words and expressions can I remember?

words   ....

expressions   ....

3   How can I practise other new words and expressions?

record them on my MP3 player ☐   write them in a notebook ☐
practise them with a friend ☐   translate them into my language ☐

4   What English have I learned outside class?

	words	expressions
on the radio		
in songs		
in films		
on the internet		
on TV		
with friends		

My Assessment Profile Unit 4

1 **What can I do? Tick (✓) the options in the table.**

⏪ = I need to study this again.   ⏸ = I'm not sure about this.   ▶ = I'm happy with this.   ⏩ = I do this very well.

		⏪	⏸	▶	⏩
Vocabulary (Student's Book pages 44 and 47)	• I can use nouns and verbs to talk about natural disasters. • I can understand and use ten phrasal verbs.				
Pronunciation (SB page 44)	• I can pronounce consonant clusters correctly.				
Reading (SB pages 45 and 50)	• I can read and understand an article about cyclones in Bangladesh and an article about a survival story.				
Grammar (SB pages 46–47 and 49)	• I can use modals to talk about ability, obligation, prohibition and advice in the present. • I can use modals to talk about ability and obligation in the past. • I can use modals to talk about possibility and certainty in the present.				
Speaking (SB page 48–49)	• I can ask for clarification.				
Listening (SB pages 48–49 and 50)	• I can understand a conversation between friends and someone giving advice.				
Writing (SB page 51)	• I can organise my writing clearly to give instructions. • I can write an information leaflet.				

2 **What new words and expressions can I remember?**

words ....

expressions ....

3 **How can I practise other new words and expressions?**

record them on my MP3 player ☐   write them in a notebook ☐
practise them with a friend ☐   translate them into my language ☐

4 **What English have I learned outside class?**

	words	expressions
on the radio		
in songs		
in films		
on the internet		
on TV		
with friends		

My Assessment Profile Unit 5

1 What can I do? Tick (✓) the options in the table.

⏪ = I need to study this again.　⏸ = I'm not sure about this.　▶ = I'm happy with this.　⏩ = I do this very well.

		⏪	⏸	▶	⏩
Vocabulary (Student's Book pages 54 and 57)	• I can use verb and noun collocations to talk about things we might see, use or do at work. • I can use adjectives and phrases to describe people's personal job qualities.				
Pronunciation (SB page 54)	• I can recognise and pronounce words with the sounds /ɜː/ and /ɔː/ correctly.				
Reading (SB pages 55 and 60)	• I can read and understand a webpage about work experience and an article about jobs of the future.				
Grammar (SB pages 56 and 59)	• I can understand when to use *will* or *going to* to talk about the future. • I can use a variety of future time phrases. • I can understand when to use the Present simple or the Present continuous to talk about the future.				
Speaking (SB pages 58–59)	• I can make a phone call. • I can leave and take a phone message.				
Listening (SB pages 58–59 and 60)	• I can understand a phone conversation and a conversation between friends.				
Writing (SB page 61)	• I can express degrees of certainty. • I can write an email about future plans.				

2 What new words and expressions can I remember?

words　..................　..................　..................　..................　..................　..................

expressions　..................　..................　..................　..................　..................

3 How can I practise other new words and expressions?

record them on my MP3 player ☐　write them in a notebook ☐

practise them with a friend ☐　translate them into my language ☐

4 What English have I learned outside class?

	words	expressions
on the radio		
in songs		
in films		
on the internet		
on TV		
with friends		

My Assessment Profile Unit 6

1   What can I do? Tick (✓) the options in the table.

⏪ = I need to study this again.   ⏸ = I'm not sure about this.   ▶ = I'm happy with this.   ⏩ = I do this very well.

		⏪	⏸	▶	⏩
Vocabulary (Student's Book pages 64 and 67)	• I can use twelve nouns to talk about things we might see at the coast. • I can use eleven verbs with the prefixes *dis-* and *re-*.				
Reading (SB pages 65 and 70)	• I can read and understand two descriptions of seaside towns and an article about a famous pirate.				
Grammar (SB pages 66 and 69)	• I can use the present, past and future passive. • I can use the passive with *by* + agent. • I can use the passive in questions.				
Pronunciation (SB page 66)	• I can understand when to use *was* with a weak or strong pronunciation.				
Speaking (SB page 68–69)	• I can ask for and give directions.				
Listening (SB pages 68–69 and 70)	• I can understand someone giving directions and a tour guide giving information.				
Writing (SB page 71)	• I can use paragraphs or sections to organise my ideas clearly. • I can write a field trip report.				

2   What new words and expressions can I remember?

words   ....

expressions   ....

3   How can I practise other new words and expressions?

record them on my MP3 player ☐   write them in a notebook ☐

practise them with a friend ☐   translate them into my language ☐

4   What English have I learned outside class?

	words	expressions
on the radio		
in songs		
in films		
on the internet		
on TV		
with friends		

My Assessment Profile Unit 7

1 What can I do? Tick (✓) the options in the table.

⏪ = I need to study this again.　⏸ = I'm not sure about this.　▶ = I'm happy with this.　⏩ = I do this very well.

		⏪	⏸	▶	⏩
Vocabulary (Student's Book pages 78 and 81)	• I can use adjective antonyms to express opposite meanings. • I can use twelve nouns to talk about space.				
Pronunciation (SB page 78)	• I can pronounce words with elided syllables correctly.				
Reading (SB pages 79 and 84)	• I can read and understand an article about places to explore on Earth and an interview with an astronomer about a space colony.				
Grammar (SB pages 80 and 83)	• I can use all forms of the First and Second conditional. • I can understand when to use the First conditional or the Second conditional. • I can use subject and object questions correctly.				
Speaking (SB pages 82–83)	• I can give warnings.				
Listening (SB pages 82–83 and 84)	• I can understand a conversation between friends and three different people talking about space colonies.				
Writing (SB page 85)	• I can use the correct layout and expressions for a formal letter. • I can write an application letter.				

2 What new words and expressions can I remember?

words ....

expressions ....

3 How can I practise other new words and expressions?

record them on my MP3 player ☐　　write them in a notebook ☐

practise them with a friend ☐　　translate them into my language ☐

4 What English have I learned outside class?

	words	expressions
on the radio		
in songs		
in films		
on the internet		
on TV		
with friends		

My Assessment Profile Unit 8

1 What can I do? Tick (✓) the options in the table.

⏪ = I need to study this again.   ⏸ = I'm not sure about this.   ▶ = I'm happy with this.   ⏩ = I do this very well.

		⏪	⏸	▶	⏩
Vocabulary (Student's Book pages 88 and 91)	• I can use twelve collocations to talk about spying. • I can form negative adjectives with the prefixes *un-*, *dis-*, *im-* and *in-*.				
Pronunciation (SB pages 88)	• I can recognise and pronounce words with the sounds /eə/, /iː/ and /eɪ/ correctly.				
Reading (SB pages 89 and 94)	• I can read and understand an extract from a spy novel and an article about surveillance in schools.				
Grammar (SB pages 90 and 93)	• I can use all forms of the Past perfect. • I can understand when to use the Past perfect or the Past simple. • I can use all forms of the Third conditional.				
Speaking (SB page 92–93)	• I can apologise and explain why I did something. • I can acknowledge someone else's explanation.				
Listening (SB pages 92–93 and 94)	• I can understand conversations between friends and family members and a report.				
Writing (SB page 95)	• I can organise my ideas into clear paragraphs. • I can use different expressions to give opinions, introduce points, and conclude. • I can write an opinion essay.				

2 What new words and expressions can I remember?

words ....

expressions ....

3 How can I practise other new words and expressions?

record them on my MP3 player ☐   write them in a notebook ☐
practise them with a friend ☐   translate them into my language ☐

4 What English have I learned outside class?

	words	expressions
on the radio		
in songs		
in films		
on the internet		
on TV		
with friends		

My Assessment Profile Unit 9

1 **What can I do? Tick (✓) the options in the table.**

⏪ = I need to study this again.　⏸ = I'm not sure about this.　▶ = I'm happy with this.　⏩ = I do this very well.

		⏪	⏸	▶	⏩
Vocabulary (Student's Book pages 98 and 101)	• I can use thirteen collocations to talk about parties. • I can use ten reporting verbs with the correct reported speech structures.				
Pronunciation (SB page 98)	• I can recognise and pronounce words with the sounds /ʃ/, /ʒ/ and /dʒ/ correctly.				
Reading (SB pages 99 and 104)	• I can read and understand an article about proms and an article about three different coming of age ceremonies.				
Grammar (SB pages 100–101 and 103)	• I can report affirmative and negative statements in different tenses using *said* and *told*. • I can report affirmative and negative commands and requests. • I can report questions.				
Speaking (SB page 102–103)	• I can make suggestions. • I can agree and disagree with suggestions.				
Listening (SB pages 102–103 and 104)	• I can understand a conversation between friends and a radio interview.				
Writing (SB page 105)	• I can use pronouns and possessive adjectives to avoid repeating ideas. • I can write a letter giving advice.				

2 **What new words and expressions can I remember?**

words ....

expressions ....

3 **How can I practise other new words and expressions?**

record them on my MP3 player ☐　　write them in a notebook ☐

practise them with a friend ☐　　translate them into my language ☐

4 **What English have I learned outside class?**

	words	expressions
on the radio		
in songs		
in films		
on the internet		
on TV		
with friends		

Pearson Education Limited,
Edinburgh Gate, Harlow
Essex, CM20 2JE, England
and Associated Companies throughout the world

www.pearsonelt.com

First published 2014
Fourth impression 2016

ISBN 978-1-4479-4366-2

Set in 10.5/12.5pt LTC Helvetica Neue Light
Printed in Slovakia by Neografia

Acknowledgements

The publisher would like to thank the following for their kind permission
to reproduce their photographs:

(Key: b-bottom; c-centre; l-left; r-right; t-top)

Action Plus Sports Images: Stephen Bartholomew 104cr; **Alamy
Images**: Dygiclick 109tr, Hermes Images 11br/3, © tomas kraus 11br/2,
Adrian Muttitt 11br/4, Gary Roebuck 112cr, Adrian Sherratt 11br/1,
Jack Sullivan 105bl, Nick Turner 104cl; **Corbis**: Citizen Stock /
© Sherrie Nickol 5l, © Macduff Everton 59bl, © Hulton-Deutsch
Collection 13tr, © Inmagine Asia 106bl, © Lauryn Ishak 59tl, © Dirk
Lindner 30tc, © Gideon Mendel 112br, © Ocean 106cl; **Fotolia.com**:
126-135; **Getty Images**: E+ / zorani 106cr, Flickr 112cl, Stone /
Britt Erlanson 112bl; **Pearson Education Ltd**: Studio 8 113cr,
Tudor Photography 113br, Jules Selmes 57cl, Steve Shott 48tr;
PhotoDisc: 84cr; **Rex Features**: Everett Collection 69tr, Mykel
Nicolaou 104bl, Ray Tang 48cl; **Shutterstock.com**: chrisdorney 59cl,
Dariush M 109br, Alexander Demyanenko 104tl, Eder 12br (a), R. Gino
Santa Maria 114b, Natali Glado 17br, Andreas Gradin 30tr, Chaikovskiy
Igor 12br (b), Iryna1 33cl, JeniFoto 49r, jjphotos 104tr, JonMilnes 109cr,
Dmitry Kalinovsky 24cr, Stanislav Komogorov 29cl, Aleksandr Markin
105tr, Mictoon 112tl, Olegusk 63br, Pressmaster 109bl, stocknadia
114t, TTphoto 109tl, ValeStock 49l; **SuperStock**: Ableimages 106tl,
age fotostock 24bl, 30tl, Belinda Images 106tr, Blend Images 10cl, 24tl,
24tr, 24br, 82c, 105cr, Corbis 53tr, Cultura Limited 23tl, 39tr, 112tr,
Cusp 39tl, Flirt 48br, Image Source 78tl, 106br, 109cl, OJO Images 45tr,
PhotoAlto 105cl, Pixtal 24cl, Tetra Images 104br, 105tl, Westend61 62tr,
Yuri Arcurs Media 75tl

Cover image: *Front*: **Superstock**: *f*Stop

All other images © Pearson Education Limited

In some instances we have been unable to trace the owners of
copyright material, and we would appreciate any information that
would enable us to do so.

Illustrated by: Chris Coady pages 21, 42, 73, 111; Julian Mosedale
pages 7, 26, 34, 38, 54, 55, 70, 72, 107, 108, 116, 119;
Paula Franco pages 20, 37, 76, 110, 121; Peskimo page 8.